BRENT PATTISON

PRAISE

The Cornerstone of Coaching to Success for Supervisors and Managers

Brent Pattison

© **Copyright 2024 – Brent Pattison**
All rights reserved.

The content contained within this book may not be reproduced, duplicated or transmitted without direct written permission from the author or the publisher.

Under no circumstances will any blame or legal responsibility be held against the publisher, or author, for any damages, reparation, or monetary loss due to the information contained within this book, either directly or indirectly.

Legal Notice:
This book is copyright protected. It is only for personal use. You cannot amend, distribute, sell, use, quote or paraphrase any part, or the content within this book, without the consent of the author or publisher.

Disclaimer Notice:
Please note the information contained within this document is for educational and entertainment purposes only. All effort has been executed to present accurate, up to date, reliable, complete information. No warranties of any kind are declared or implied. Readers acknowledge that the author is not engaging in the rendering of legal, financial, medical or professional advice. The content within this book has been derived from various sources. Please consult a licensed professional before attempting any techniques outlined in this book.

By reading this document, the reader agrees that under no circumstances is the author responsible for any losses, direct or indirect, that are incurred as a result of the use of information contained within this document, including, but not limited to, errors, omissions, or inaccuracies.

Praise for Those Who Made this Book Possible

After 2 years of writing, editing, re-writing. Sending out drafts to my valuable test readers. More reading & researching. Completely revising the structure of the book. More writing again, editing again. More interviews. More writing. Sending out to more people to help edit and give feedback. I finally have produced a book that I believe captures the essence of the foundational skills of coaching which support being both a good leader and a good manager.

Of course, as a book about PRAISE being the cornerstone skill of the foundation for good coaching, I must give praise to those who helped me on my journey. Unfortunately, I'm breaking one of my own 3Ps of good Praise – in many cases this praise isn't prompt – but I hope I make up for it with precision and personalization.

First, thank you to all the people whom I've had the pleasure of working with. The people I've reported to, the customers I served, my peers and especially the people who honored me with the privilege and responsibility of supporting them as their leader. Those are the people who allowed me to make mistakes. To learn from them. Patiently participating in my training sessions – usually about coaching with the 3Ps of Business in mind. And most importantly – allowing me to be a part of their success. I am truly grateful to have had that opportunity to learn from so many of you.

To Dale Carnegie for writing 'How to Win Friends and Influence People'. To Napoleon Hill for writing 'Think and Grow Rich'. To

Earl Nightingale for recording 'The Strangest Secret'. To the team of authors of 'Crucial Conversations'. To Stephen Covey for writing '7 Habits of Highly Effective People'. To Lee Iaccoca for sharing inspiring leadership lessons including his 3Ps of Business Operations. And to the other dozens (hundreds?) of authors and leaders who have publicly shared their leadership, management and general stories of human ingenuity, innovation and inspiration.

To Doug Jones, Dick Eichner, Rob Yarmo – thank you for your mentorship. While delivered from vastly different perspectives – and in many cases with many years in between, you each have demonstrated kindness, professionalism and have my heartfelt respect and gratitude.

To Deborah Lewis, who although we had not worked together previously, willingly shared her time and some amazing stories of people leadership and the power of providing supportive feedback. Thank you for sharing how you consistently created customer-centric cultures within the businesses you supported.

To Marci Carris, whose valuable mentorship and leadership while my client, has continued well past our time working together. Thank you for sharing so many valuable insights and experiences from your inspired career. And of course, thank you for your valuable review and recommended edits to the final draft of this book.

To Seth Silver, whose father Harvey was an early leadership mentor of mine and Seth, you picked up where Harvey left off. Seth is the co-author of 'Meaningful Partnerships At Work', a book that illustrates many of the key leadership qualities I'm hopefully accurately incorporating into my own book. Seth, thank you for the countless hours of advice, opinions and helpful feedback along the way. I'm in your debt.

To my Aunt Caroline, who in addition to always being a supportive family member, provided an extensive edit of my first draft of this book. Thank you for helping me identify my many bad writing habits, and hopefully improving the readability of this book. Any errors remaining are definitely mine though, where I missed her suggestions or didn't follow her advice.

To David Clements, my former colleague and close friend, who also extensively reviewed the first draft of the book, and intently listened to me outline my model for business success. Dave, thank you for challenging me to improve upon it, strengthening the model, and as a result, for being a major contributor to the framework and ideas contained within this book.

To my niece Ryan, who was an early first reader of the first edition of this book, thank you for being a constantly supportive cheerleader, always positively encouraging me along the way.

To my nephew Carter, who has had to endure many iterations of the content in this book. Thank you for all the times I sent texts of logos, images, ideas, quotes – and every time, you provided your unique and valuable, and often entertaining insights and perspective.

To my extraordinarily supportive friends – Mr. Livingston, Mr. Gardner, Mr. Norley, Mr. Baughman, Mr. Ryan, Mr. Noel, Mr. Whissell, Mr. Sleep and Ms. Knight. You have all provided me with your unique guidance, support, feedback and more. I will do my best to always be there to provide the same.

To my kids, Turner and Sadie. You both inspire me every day. You make me proud every day. I'm especially proud of how both

Brent Pattison

of you are consistently kind and polite to everyone you meet. I'm so grateful to have had the pleasure of watching you both grow up into the uniquely inspiring young adults you have become.

And of course, last but not least, to my wife of two decades, my partner in life for three, Catherine. Thank you for sharing your life with me, for supporting me while I wrote this book, and for raising our wonderful children.

Love you all.

Brent

Table of Contents

Preface - Purpose of this Book 8

Chapter 1: Introduction 12

Chapter 2: The Business Success Pyramid 16

Chapter 3: The 3P System of Coaching - An Introduction 47

Chapter 4: 1st P of COACHING – PREPARE 59

Chapter 5: PRESENT 83

Chapter 6: PRAISE 103

Chapter 7: Frequency & Duration of Coaching 127

Chapter 8: Correction Conversations 135

Chapter 9: Connection through Coaching & The 3P Success Pyramid 140

Preface - Purpose of this Book

What's the problem it solves?

- You've been promoted or want to get promoted into a leadership role. It answers the question "How do I be a good boss so I can keep getting promoted and not mess up this opportunity?"

What's the Result it achieves?

- This book can teach you some simple steps to make your team succeed under your leadership, paving the way to your continued career growth - regardless of education or experience.

What's the Process it teaches?

1. Understanding the basic keys to success for ANY business and any leader in any management role
2. How to properly COACH employees to achieve performance for your team

3. Know when to CORRECT vs Coach - and how to do it EFFECTIVELY to improve performance and not piss off employees

How does it help teach it faster?

- You can learn from experience (takes a long time) *or*
- You can learn from your boss (even assuming they are GREAT, still will take a LONG time) *or*
- You can learn from reading a bunch of leadership books. But which ones (of the hundreds of thousands available) are good for you specifically? Especially if you don't like reading! *or*
- You can learn from my 25 years of practical leadership & all my investments in the best leadership training available & and all my mistakes in this short & simple book.

Ultimately, to TRANSFORM yourself into a GOOD leader, achieve better performance for your team & advance your career.

Who's My Target Audience?

What Pains & Problems Do They Have?

- While there are many good leadership books, not many provide practical systems that an individual can apply to their current role
- They don't know how to deal with employees to make them want to do better and improve
- Understanding the difference between being a boss vs being co-workers with people
- Dealing with their own shitty boss
- They hate reading impractical books & taking courses

What Obstacles Must They Overcome?

- LOTS of information on how to be a good leader/good boss, but don't know where to start
- Many books and courses teach high-level concepts vs practical how-to's
- They hate reading books & taking courses

What skills are they looking to Acquire?

- Be an effective communicator
- Be a good coach
- Be a good boss that people want to work for
- Better manage their time

What are they going through right now?

- Learning on the fly and making mistakes, including pissing off good employees
- Not making the most out of their time
- Not improving their team's performance as quickly as they need to
- Not receiving direction and coaching from their own boss on how to be an effective leader

Chapter 1: Introduction

I spent nearly 25 years in corporate leadership roles, starting as a supervisor, and working my way up the corporate ladder to manager, then senior manager, director, vice president, and senior vice president. I fostered relationships with Fortune100 companies, built teams as large as 4000 front-line employees, which were supported by 350 supervisors, 50 managers, and 15 senior managers, directors, and vice presidents. In addition to running operations teams, I've led HR, Recruiting, Leadership Training, and Resource Planning teams for a company with 35,000 employees scattered across the globe. Now I run my own consulting business, helping transform businesses from good to great using systems and processes I learned and innovated upon, to help entrepreneurs achieve their unique vision of success.

So why this book?

First, I've always held a firm belief that the people in the role of 'supervisor' or whatever title a company gives this role, whether in a small company of 25 employees or a large company of 25,000, these folks are often the most under-appreciated group in an organization.

One, it's a hard job! You still need to be an expert at whatever task the team you are leading is doing. In fact, if Suzy on the team calls in sick today, her supervisor may have to do Suzy's job for the day – in addition to doing their regular job of supporting the rest of the team.

Two, they are the first group to hear and deal with all the problems and challenges from the front-line employees AND deal with whatever shit has rolled down-hill from 'upper-management'.

Three, in many cases, especially in industries where the front-line employees have an opportunity to earn bonuses or commissions, the supervisor, who previously was one of the top-performing front-line employees, may earn *less* than they did as a front-line employee, because of giving up their performance bonuses.

Four, supervisors are often left to figure out for themselves how to become a 'good boss' and learn how to be an effective leader, let alone learn the skills of 'time management'. I've been in leadership roles for over 25 years and I'm still learning and making mistakes in both of those key areas.

So why would anyone want this job? Everyone has their own personal reasons, but the most common reason I've found from interviewing and talking to thousands of front-line leaders is it's the first big step in their path of career development. It's the first step to getting practical leadership experience to advance their own personal development. This book is a simple tool to help someone on this path advance that goal a bit faster.

The other reason I wrote this book is I've always been passionate about developing my own leadership skills. I've attended dozens of seminars, read a multitude of books, watched weeks' worth of YouTube, joined Toastmasters including co-founding the world's top club focused on leadership development, and written and delivered a wide range of presentations and speeches about leadership. The reality is, there is no quick and easy way to become an excellent leader, nor is there one **right** way to lead. For someone new to the role of a supervisor or manager, the single most impactful skill they can learn to do well, to work towards success and start their own path of leadership development is to work at being a better coach.

As with all things about being a good leader, there is of course no **single, right** way to coach, either. I have worked directly with thousands of leaders and observed and evaluated tens of thousands of coaching plans and sessions. I've utilized many different coaching software tools, including advanced tools employing AI and I've also led the design and build of two custom coaching software tools. I've seen what works, and what doesn't. I've made many mistakes, so you don't have to.

Why is coaching so difficult? Because there is a long list of different situations that require different methods of coaching. Becoming good at coaching in all different situations for all different types of people takes learning and innovating through experience and evaluation.

In this book, I've attempted to summarize the best coaching models, techniques, and skills that I've witnessed succeed for the thousands of people I've had the privilege of working with over the course of my career.

The 3Ps of Coaching can help transform you into a good leader, achieve better performance for your team and advance your career by providing a simple foundation of what makes ANY business successful and outlining the fundamental steps to providing coaching for the employees you as a manager or supervisor are there to support.

Chapter 2:
The Business Success Pyramid

What was your first job - not counting the house chores your parents made you do - what was your first actual job? Did you have a boss to teach you and coach you, or did you have to figure it out on your own?

My first job was as a paperboy - this was when people had the newspaper delivered to their door daily. I had a nice route of about 25 houses close to my home. Honestly, I have no clue who trained me or how I learned the job. The only coaching or feedback I got was from the customers I served. What I do remember is that I was committed to being damn good at it. I was going to do it well!

Every day, when I got home from school, I'd have a stack of papers sitting at the end of my driveway. Before I could deliver them though, I first had to stuff the accompanying ads and flyers into the newspapers - Saturdays also meant stuffing the comics in as well. I worked hard to develop the fastest possible assembly line for myself in my driveway to get those flyers stuffed into each newspaper as quickly as I could, then load the assembled product into my delivery bag.

Once my delivery bag was set to go, I hopped on my bike and rode down my route. Every day was like a challenge to beat my time from the day before - without sacrificing quality to those customers I needed to impress.

I learned quickly that in addition to the ridiculously small cut of the weekly fee I had to collect from customers every Saturday (no hourly wage for paperboys) if my customers liked the service, they'd add a tip just for me. I also learned that the key to maximum profitability was creating an optimal balance between efficiency and effectiveness.

That meant I shouldn't ride my bike right up a customer's laneway to their door - that would be rude. I shouldn't drop my bike while hopping off in a rush to cut time off my route without care, then I'd maybe damage someone's lawn while running to the door. I needed to ensure when stuffing flyers in haste, that I didn't rip, tear or smudge things in the process. I needed to learn which customers preferred it under a mat, placed in-between a screen and wood door, or placed in a mailbox.

Then came collection day. I learned that the more courteous, friendly, and outgoing I was while collecting the fee (yeah, customers used to have to give me the cash or check that paid for their paper, and then I had to pay the newspaper), that my tips grew. I discovered it was better to show up for collection day wearing my nicer clothes and being properly presentable. I learned that this interaction with my customers was a good opportunity to learn their preferences, how I could serve them better, and get their feedback - or an 'evaluation' of my service. I also learned the value of giving my customers praise during these interactions. Telling them specifically how much I appreciated the opportunity to deliver their paper to them every day, made them happier customers!

Ultimately, the collecting role helped me make connections with my customers. While investing a bit more time in chatting up my customers to give them praise made the 'job' take longer, it resulted in greater profits for my business.

To offset a greater investment of time in creating the customer experience, I continuously thought of ideas to speed up my prep work: a better knife to open the plastic that wrapped the papers, and created optimal page opening techniques. I also worked on improved strategies to cut down my delivery time; I identified improved locations for jumping off my bike, found better routes between houses, and not to mention just biking faster. At the same time, I continued memorizing the preferences of my customers and providing an overall better experience for both how they received the papers and how I made my collections.

Eventually, I passed off my paper route when a job with more opportunity came my way (whoo! Dishwasher!!!), but the primary lessons of doing the job well - creating a balance between efficiency and effectiveness through continuous learning, constant innovation and creating a connection with my customers – and that doing the job well created an improved result for me and my profits has stuck with me since then.

The reason I did OK came down to a self-driving motivation to do a good job. Of course, if I had had a good coach or mentor, that would have been way better, but I focused on learning from my own experiences, constantly innovating to improve both effectiveness and efficiency, which resulted in better connections with my customers. My paper route experience provided an early understanding of the building blocks of a successful business. And a reminder that having a good coach would have sped this process up significantly!

The 3P Business Success Pyramid

Just as no two people are the same, no two businesses are the same. Every single business is completely unique. Even for large organizations with many locations, each location is a little bit different. McDonald's, arguably one of the most iconic representations of a successful chain that delivers a consistent product regardless of location – is going to be at least slightly different from one location to another.

This may be a good place to stop and define exactly what is a business. The simplest definition: A business is the exchange of MONEY for the PERCEIVED VALUE of a product or service.

Which means, customers will only give their money to a business where that PERCEIVED VALUE is greater than the amount of money they pay for that product or service. (For the rest of this book, we'll use the term PRODUCT to universally refer to a product or a service).

In turn, this means for a business to be successful, it's all about the CUSTOMER EXPERIENCE. For a business to be successful, it's customers must remain happy with this exchange. Business Success = Customer Happiness. I'll repeat this one more time, the customer must receive perceived value greater than the amount of money they pay for the product.

You've likely heard terms like "customer-centric", "customer-obsessed", "all about the customer" when many businesses describe themselves – well this is why. Without customers happy to trade their cash, there can't be a business.

So, what makes up a business? EVERY business is made up of the same 3 things:

The PEOPLE that make up the organization (employees, partners, team members including yourself).

The outcomes or PRODUCT of the combined actions of the team (customer products or services).

And the results or PROFIT that allows the organization to continue and thrive.

While every business is made up of these same 3 things, no two businesses will have an identical make-up of their People, Product & Profit.

Now let's imagine SUCCESS for a business as a pyramid. We've established that business success = customer success/a great customer experience/customer happiness. As the primary ingredients of a business - PEOPLE,

PRODUCT, and PROFIT – they represent the top of the pyramid of business success (ie. Customer success). Your business can't be stable and successful unless you ensure all three are equally balanced. There is also a direct relationship between them. If your people are happy, they'll create a better product for your customers, if your customers are happy they'll keep buying your product, which will help create profits for your business, as your business creates profits, it can re-invest into making it's people happier, making more and better products, creating more profits, etc, etc, etc.

The survival and success of any organization come down to those three things - People, Product, and Profits. The first time I saw the concept, it was attributed to the former CEO of both Ford and Chrysler, Lee Iacocca, who helped revive and possibly saved Chrysler from extinction in the 1980's - to quote Mr. Iacocca, "In the end, all business operations can be reduced to three words: people, product and profits", he also added, "People come first". It's your people who will interact with the customers you sell your product or service to, and if your people aren't happy, your product won't be represented well, and as a result, your organization and profits will suffer because your customers won't keep buying.

I want to reinforce that all three P's, are equally important. If you don't have customers to buy your product, you won't have profits, which means you can't have any people working in the business...take care of your People first, but Product & Profits are equally important to keep your organization in existence.

PEOPLE - Whether a business has 1 employee or 10,000, without people, the business cannot exist. There will be no product or services, therefore no customers can buy anything, which means no profits to continue the business. A business needs to have and KEEP happy employees.

PRODUCT - The 'product' is not just the item or services customers buy. The product is every part of the customer experience. How easy you make it to buy, the quality of the service received before, during and after buying - that is the product of a business. A business needs to have and keep happy customers.

PROFIT - Profits are the fuel that keeps a business running. It doesn't matter if it's a non-profit or volunteer organization either. If you spend more money than you bring in, the company will cease to exist. A business needs to be profitable.

As we discuss the layers that support a business, always remember that incorporating a focus on all the 3Ps of Business into every action you take is the key to keeping any business going.

I'm going to repeat this again. There is a deep relationship between the 3Ps of every business. The people working in the business need to be happy to create and deliver a good product. A good business ensures that the people working in the business are happy. A good business also ensures it defines and shares clear expectations for every employee, precisely how their work will increase the value of the product of the business. Happy employees create a better product that creates happier customers. Happy customers translate into profits, which of course makes for happy investors (especially if that investor an entrepreneur). This results in the investors re-investing profits into supporting the people, to create an even better product – and repeat.

When you really look at the 3Ps of Business, of every business – those 3Ps are serving different groups of people – the *people* working in the business creating the product for the *people* who buy the product, to create profit for the *people* who took the risk to invest in the business. Business is made of people serving people.

The happier the people working in the business, the better the product for making customers happier, which creates more profit to make investors happy, more profit, happier people working in the business, etc., etc., etc. A continuous circle.

Why We Work

The answer to this question is going to be slightly different for everyone. However, why each of us works is based on a mix of these 4 things:

1. Cash – We need money to pay the bills, to keep us safe and secure, to keep a roof over our heads and food in our bellies. We need this cash flow to do the things we like and buy the comforts that make us happy.
2. Build Value – We want to have something of value to be put to future use, perhaps to pass down to our families, to create a legacy of our efforts.
3. Create Free Time – Having enough cash and value stored up allows us the freedom to choose how we spend our time. The more secure our cash flow and store of value, the more flexible we can be with how we choose to spend our time.
4. Fulfill Meaning – For many of us, we work because of some internal drive to fulfill a purpose, to give us meaning.

What mix of those 4 things is important to you, along with a mix of your skills and experience will determine one of two paths to achieving them through one of two types of work – a job or starting your own business. Some people may do both at different times in their life, or even at the same time.

If we want to increase our CASH, VALUE, TIME or MEANING – whether in a job or running a business we will need to become a BOSS of some type. Being a great boss doesn't require you to be the boss of other people (although it often does) – even if you are only the boss of one - yourself

- it essentially takes the same skills as being a boss of others to be a great boss.

As a GREAT boss in a business – a business made up of the 3Ps of Business – People, Product & Profit – you will need to become excellent at doing two things – LEADING and MANAGING, to support the business.

Now if you've spent any amount of time listening to "experts" about leadership, perhaps you've heard things like "Be a Leader, not a Boss", or "Leaders are preferred over Managers". Most of this advice is well-intended but misses the point. There are *good* leaders, and *bad* leaders. There are *good* managers and *bad* managers. There are *good* bosses, and *bad* bosses.

It's all about being a good boss – regardless of the title assigned to the job. And a truly *great* boss is both a *great* leader <u>AND</u> a *great* manager.

Let me illustrate with a story.

Once upon a time there were two farmers – Larry and Mike.

Larry was an exceptional leader. He had complete clarity of his purpose. He farmed to provide food to feed the entire community and he shared his vision for the farm with both the people that worked on his farm and with his customers. He led with a deep understanding of principles, principles on how to treat other people well, always giving praise and showing respect for people and never sacrificing his integrity to make a buck. And he led with a true sense of progress, always striving to improve, to be better and better at everything he did.

Mike, now this guy was an amazing manager. He had a knack for making clear plans, he had a long-term 10-year plan, a 3-year plan a one-year plan, and a specific plan for each and every season of the year. Not only did he have well-written plans, he nailed down all the best processes to maximize the growth of his crops, how to use his tools and equipment most effectively, and clear processes to train new farm employees. He also had all the right performance measurements to track and report the performance of all the activities on the farm to optimally grow his crops.

Unfortunately, both Larry and Mike failed at farming and had to sell their farms. See, while Larry was a great leader, he lacked any of Mike's management skills. And while Mike was an exceptional manager, he didn't have any of Larry's leadership talent. Perhaps if they partnered together, they could have learned from each other or worked together to be great bosses but without being BOTH a great leader and a great manager, neither were able to make their business successful.

To be a great boss – of one or many – requires you to be both a great leader AND a great manager.

Going back to our representation of business success as a pyramid, the 3Ps of the business (people, product, profit) are supported, by the 3Ps of Leadership **AND** the 3Ps of Management.

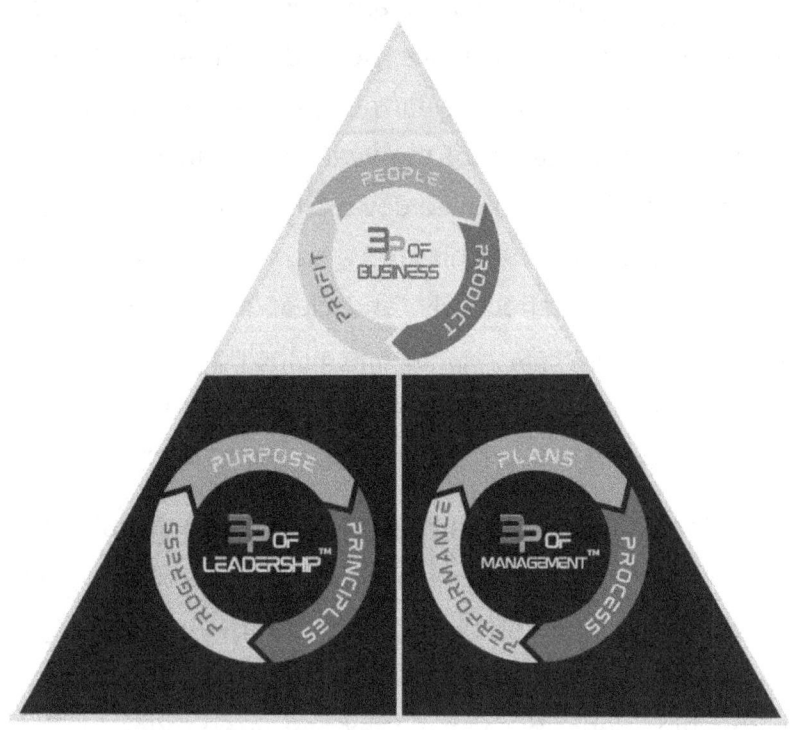

The 3Ps of LEADERSHIP

This book is NOT going to be a deep dive into the extremely important subject of leadership and leadership philosophy. There are hundreds of **thousands** of books on this subject and if you're reading this book, you bought it to learn the ESSENTIALS of becoming a good leader – specifically, how to coach effectively.

Yet, understanding the core elements of leadership can you put on a path to understanding how to be a good boss, including how to coach.

As illustrated above, the 3Ps of Leadership are focused on three core elements – all with one goal in mind – inspiring people. The people that make up the business. The people working in the business, the people who buy and use the product of the business and the people who invested in the business who depend on the profits of the business.

What are the 3Ps of Leadership?

PURPOSE - Leading with purpose means you start with an understanding of your "why". Why are you trying to lead? What is the purpose you are trying to achieve? From your purpose, you can craft a Vision and a Mission to share with the people you lead and the customers you want to help.

PRINCIPLES - Principles are objective universal truths that transcend cultures and individuals. By understanding the principles of human nature most important to you, you can share the personal **VALUES** that make up how you will lead others. The more aligned your values are with those universal principles, the more effective a leader you can be.

PROGRESS - The root word in 'leadership' is 'lead'. To lead others, you are leading them in a direction. An effective leader moves in a positive, upward or forward direction. To be an effective leader, your intention must be to lead with progress in mind.

1st P of Leadership - PURPOSE - Start With Why

I didn't have a clearly defined purpose for my paper route business written down, but I knew I wanted to be the best paperboy possible. I have since learned a few things that may have helped me become even better at creating that clarity of purpose.

One of the most viewed Ted Talks of all time is by Simon Sinek, titled "Start with Why". Sinek is one of the most respected voices on the subject of leadership and success today.

One of the reasons it's such a popular video is because it speaks clearly about what makes an organization or a person successful. Personally, I think it is a great place to start if you are trying to define a vision for an organization or for yourself.

https://www.youtube.com/watch?v=u4ZoJKF_VuA&ab_channel=TEDxTalks

Sinek uses an image to describe what he feels makes organizations successful, something he calls the Golden Circle.

My interpretation of Sinek's Golden Circle is that any organization - a business, a kid's sports team, a community - needs to start with a purpose - a WHY. Whether you are a team of one or a team of thousands if there is no purpose, there is nothing to strive for - you can't clearly define how or what your organization does or is. It is having clarity of purpose that drives our behaviours and decisions. The more clearly we understand that purpose, our why, the more intentional focus we'll be able to bring to our actions.

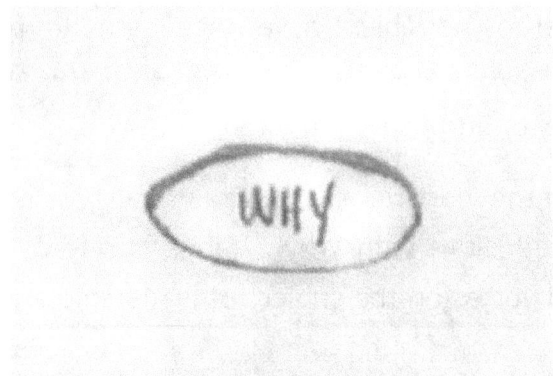

Once you have a purpose, you can define a mission - how you are going to accomplish things in the now and near future aligned with that purpose.

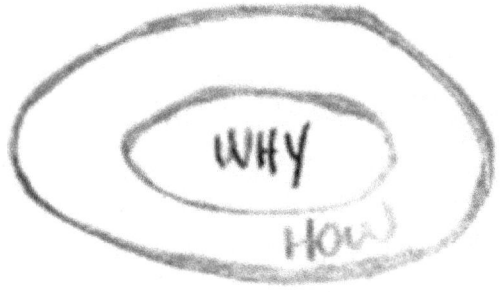

Now that you have a clearly defined purpose - the why, and a mission - the how - it makes it much easier to define what your organization is - what service, product, or result is being strived for, including a long-term one - in other words, a vision. Your unique vision of success.

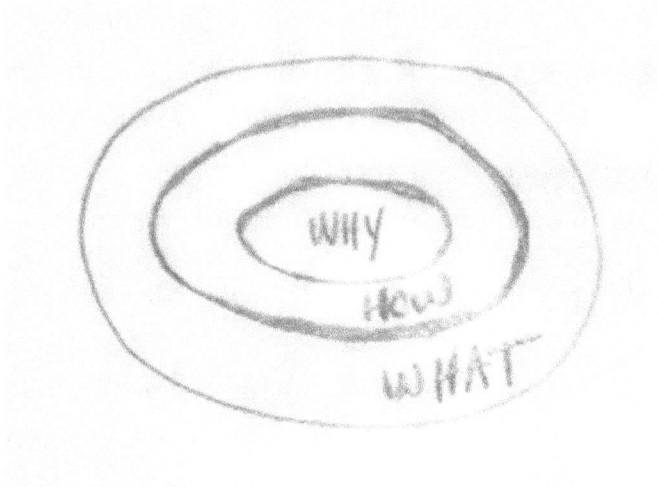

Sinek provides a strong case for defining your organization with this golden circle and I highly recommend watching his video or reading his book, Start With Why. Understanding your why is essential to defining your *purpose*, the first P of Leadership.

2nd P of Leadership - PRINCIPLES - Taking it beyond the Golden Circle

For any organization – starting with an understanding of your purpose, by clearly stating your mission – is what helps you define a unique vision of success.

Defining values that are important to how you will lead others is extremely important. Defined and *shared* values help reinforce the type of culture that exists among the team members of the organization as you work together toward achieving your Purpose as defined by the Mission and Vision. Some organizations may refer to them as 'Core Values', or perhaps they describe them as 'Core Behaviours', or 'Rules of Engagement' even. Bottom line, values are how people work together, go about doing their work. They are the bonds that create a culture within an organization.

The Values of an organization or an individual are the outward representation of personally held beliefs based upon universal principles of human nature most significant to the success of that business or individual. By universal human principles I'm referring to things like:

- APPRECIATION
- RECIPROCITY
- RESPECT
- DIGNITY
- HONESTY
- KINDNESS
- INTEGRITY
- HUMILITY
- COURAGE
- EXCELLENCE
- FAIRNESS
- RESPONSIBILITY

Defining shared values based on PRINCIPLES that you, as the leader can demonstrate daily, is important if you want others - employees, customers, and investors - to buy into your mission & vision. These values become the support and glue that helps you keep these groups connected to your mission and vision and ultimately, your purpose. By aligning your Mission, Vision, and Purpose through shared core values based upon universal human principles is how you can set yourself up for success.

Vision vs Mission vs Purpose vs Values (MVVP) based on Principles

Remember - we should start with why if we're going to be successful. While I didn't define this for myself as a paperboy, my purpose could have been...

Purpose - WHY doing this thing is important

Paperboy Purpose: People need their daily newspaper to stay connected with current events.

Values – Your deeply held beliefs that guide your choices and behaviours aligned with the principles of human nature

Paperboy Values: On-time. Right location. Integrity. Respect.

Mission - HOW I am currently working towards that purpose

Paperboy Mission: To deliver the KW Record to my customers on time and delivered to the right location every day.

To help define your vision - be it for yourself or even an organization - try using the 'THE, FOR, WHO' formula.

Define and refine what exactly is the 'THE' - specifically, your combined team of PEOPLE (even if just you).

Then specify who it is 'FOR' - who is your target customer, the recipient of the PRODUCT resulting from the combined actions of the team.

Lastly, specifically when you define 'WHO', define what the expected outcomes and benefits are for that audience, and why your product is the best. Your true "unique value proposition" will ultimately get you the results or PROFITS needed to keep the organization going.

Paperboy Vision - To be **THE** best paperboy **FOR** New Hamburg's subscribers of the KW record **WHO** want their news delivered on time the way they want it.

3rd P of Leadership - PROGRESS – Leading your MVVP in the right direction

To be a success, there needs to be a leader to define, communicate and ultimately connect the actions of the team to that mission, vision, values, and purpose. Always supporting the 3Ps of Business equally - PEOPLE, PRODUCT, PROFIT - is key to creating and ultimately achieving a mission and vision. For that to happen, there needs to be a leader that connects them and keeps all three of the 3Ps of business equally stable and healthy. A good leader ensures everyone - paperboys and their customers, employees and supervisors, owners of a business and suppliers, understand their connection to each other, and to the mission, vision, values, defined by **PURPOSE**, built upon **PRINCIPLES** that define what success looks like and guiding how the MVVP is communicated, and moving forward with **PROGRESS** towards that unique vision of success. Whether you're a team of many or a team of one - it requires leadership.

To lead with progress means to think about how it can be done better. To have a growth mindset. To challenge the status quo, to look for ways to innovate, and to inspire others to innovate for the better.

I'm not the owner – why do I care about PURPOSE, PRINCIPLES & PROGRESS?

Let's say you and your friend just got jobs at McDonald's and you both get to start by flipping burgers. You both are equally talented at following the training provided by the crew trainer, and you're both equally competent burger flippers. In this scenario, you don't really care about why you're there, except to earn your paycheck and not get fired.

Your friend however, decides it's important to understand why he's flipping the burgers and makes an effort to understand that the company's core values are "**we place the customer experience at the core of all we do, we are committed to our people, we believe in the McDonald's system, we operate our business ethically,** we give back to our communities, we grow our business profitably, and we strive continually to improve.", and that their mission is **"to be our customers' favorite place and way to eat and drink."**

He even learns that McDonald's vision is "to move with velocity to drive profitable growth and become an even better McDonald's serving more customers delicious food each day around the world" (Note, McDonald's may or may not have followed my recommended strategy or used the same definitions to differentiate Vision & Mission).

Now honestly ask yourself - who is going to end up working harder to serve more customers, who is going to ensure customers like the quality of the burgers being made, and who is going to ultimately perform better? Who is going to be the first to get promoted from the grill to the cash, to be the next crew trainer, team lead, manager? Likely not the guy who is just trying not to get fired.

The Company I Work for has a Mission, Vision, Values & Purpose (MVVP) I can agree with

Great! This makes things WAY easier! The better you can align yourself and the job you're responsible for with the stated MVVP of the company you are already working for – the more successful you'll be. As you go about your job, make sure you are aligning that MVVP with the 3Ps of the business and incorporating the 3Ps of leadership into how you perform your job. Balance the act of keeping your people happy, deliver the quality of the product (or service) being provided to customers at or above their expectations and be keenly aware how you are positively impacting the profitability of the company to keep it running smoothly – and you're launching with a head start!

The Company I work for has NO stated Mission, Vision, Values & Purpose

That's OK! This is a great opportunity to define a purpose and principles for how you will do your job - whether you're in a leadership position today or not. Remember - ALL successful businesses balance the 3Ps of Business (People, Product & Profit) and successful leaders incorporate the 3Ps of Leadership (Purpose, Principles and Progress) in how they lead themselves. Incorporate that into your OWN defined purpose and principles. Share your purpose and principles with your boss. Openly share how you are going to approach your job to ensure you are doing what you can to make the people you work with happy & satisfied. Even if you aren't in a management position, you still can have an impact on the other people you work with. Leadership is not only defined or determined by your role or title. Demonstrating leadership through contributing to making your co-workers happy, making customers happy, and having a positive impact on the financial health of your company – regardless of your role or title - will be key to your next promotion!

The Company I work for has a stated Mission, Vision, Values & Purpose - but I think it SUCKS!

Ideal situation? No. Impossible situation? Not at all. Again - if you are doing your job by keeping the people you work with happy, keeping your customers happy, and helping the company make money to keep things moving forward - no matter how poorly crafted a company's MVVP is, you can still have a positive impact. If you are doing your thing aligned with positively impacting the 3Ps of Business - I would be surprised by any company that wouldn't appreciate your contributions.

No Matter What - Take Positive Action – PROGRESS!

While I think it's important to be aligned with a company's purpose, vision, mission, and values or to define purpose and principles for yourself and your own role, it shouldn't stop you from taking action. All these things - even your purpose - may change over time. The best way to discover, refine and improve your purpose and principles is to take action!

You need to create a bias-for-action for yourself, otherwise, you will spend all your time thinking of what you want to become, without ever actually doing anything.

I think back to when I was that pretty decent paperboy - I didn't have a stated Mission, Vision, Values, or Purpose, nor did I have any clue if the newspaper I delivered for had these things defined either - I just got to doing my job. However, I can reflect back, and man, I would have been even better if I did understand the 3Ps of Leadership – PURPOSE, PRINCIPLES and PROGRESS - to align myself with my daily job! But the basic lesson of just doing it and doing it well - that my customers were happy, that I was happy doing it, and both the newspaper and I were making money if I kept my customers - was a good starting point.

I've observed that clarity comes from taking action. While you may encounter errors, make mistakes, and follow paths that aren't aligned with your purpose and principles, it is through taking action that you gain the greatest insights. The mistakes you make serve as steppingstones toward improvement.

It's also important to stop and **reflect** consistently – monthly or at least quarterly - on what worked and what didn't - and adjust, re-define, refine, and take action again - but only thinking about what you should do doesn't allow you to do any of that. Act - do something, take action.

To quote the classic motivational speaker, Earl Nightingale, "Ideas are worthless unless we act on them"!

3Ps of Management

Being a good leader – a leader who has a PURPOSE, understands human PRINCIPLES and leads with PROGRESS is only half of the requirement of being a good boss that supports the 3Ps of a business. Flip back to the story of our two farmers, Larry and Mike if you need a reminder! A good boss who supports the 3Ps of Business – it's People, Product and Profits – also needs to have good management skills in addition to understanding the 3Ps of Leadership.

Again, there are hundreds of thousands of books about management. There are thousands of well-established theories of management from all corners of the world. While I can't sit here and tell you I've studied every last one of them, I can share with you a simple model of the **most** important management elements I've observed in every successful business that I've been a part of and what I personally used to grow a business unit from start-up to over 4000 happy employees across 6 different countries, that worked together to make happy customers AND make profits:

The 3Ps of Management: PLANNING, PROCESSES & PERFORMANCE measurement.

PLANNING - Businesses need a plan. Hopefully the plan includes a written down vision, with a mission that is translated to specific long, medium and short-term goals. Goals that adhere to the S.M.A.R.T. goal-setting framework: Specific, Measurable, Attainable, Relevant and Timebound. You need a plan for you and your people to follow. To quote one of the greatest baseball players and coaches to ever walk onto a baseball diamond - "If you don't know where you're going, you might not get there."—Yogi Berra. More importantly, building a plan teaches essential planning skills. It's these planning skills that allow successful managers to pivot and adapt when obstacles inevitably fall into their path. Planning is how we turn dreams into goals, to define the actionable steps, which will help us achieve those goals, aligned with our plan.

PROCESS - Your business processes should create great employee and customer experiences while still ensuring the business is profitable. Using the right tools, how effective and efficient your processes are, and how well documented they are, determines the success of your business. Every good business will have clearly defined processes for how they do marketing to attract new customers, processes to sell to those potential customers, processes to onboard and deliver their product to those customers and processes to support those customers. Good businesses will also have specified processes for how they hire, train, support, and coach their employees. Good businesses will have processes to ensure they analyze, evaluate, and deliver profits from the business to the owners & investors of the business. Providing recurring 1:1 Performance Coaching is one of those processes that great businesses all have in place.

PERFORMANCE - Doesn't matter if you call them metrics or KPIs, if you aren't consistently measuring the numbers related to success for your People, Product and Profits, you won't know what Processes to fix nor if you are on track to achieve your Plan. A clear scorecard that is reviewed consistently, will ensure that a business stays on track to achieve its 'Unique Vision of Success'.

I thought this was a book about coaching?

It is! Ultimately coaching is the single most important leadership AND management activity you will do in the role of a supervisor or manager. This means before you start coaching, you should know the foundations of what it takes to make a business successful, in order to be good at coaching in a business. You should think exactly about WHY you are coaching, HOW you are going to coach, WHAT type of coach you will be, and what values you will represent as a coach. Defining your MVVP as a coach to your team by applying the 3Ps of Leadership **and** the 3Ps of Management. In addition, it's essential the coaching you deliver positively benefits all three of the Ps of Business - the people you're coaching, the product you are trying to improve for your customers, and the profitability of the organization you are coaching for.

Coaching is the key support layer for supporting good leadership and good management that supports the success of a business.

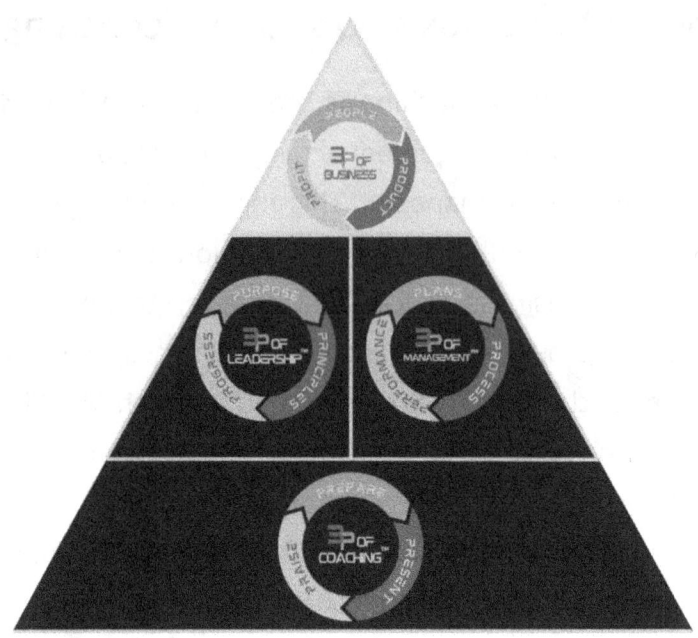

In the next chapter, we'll break down how to provide coaching as a leader and manager in a business.

Chapter 3: The 3P System of Coaching - An Introduction

When I was 25, I had been managing call center operations teams for a while and my team was doing a great job for the company and my boss asked me to attend my very first sales pitch meeting with a new potential client.

I prepare all week. I put on my best suit, I mean I was looking slick, cufflinks, $75 silk tie, the whole show!. I greeted those potential clients with exuberant confidence.

The meeting went pretty darn good, I answered every question thrown my way with precision. After the meeting, I was still pumped at the whole thing and the sales manager called me into his office.

"Brent, I appreciated how prepared you were and how skillfully you answered their questions. But, why didn't you have a notebook with you?". "Pardon?", I say.

He says "You didn't have a way to take notes. Don't you realize the kind of message that sends to a person? What if they said something meaningful? If you're going to attend an important meeting like that in the future, you have a way to take notes!".

"Please don't come unprepared to a meeting like that the next time."

I was a little taken aback. Here I was, thinking I had performed exceptionally and was going to get praise and this guy is giving me shit! But I quickly realized he had a point. Why didn't I bring a notebook? There were a few things said during the meeting I wish I had written down. I thanked him for the feedback and slunk back to my cubicle.

That happened to me 25 years ago, and it was one of the best lessons I ever learned. And while yes, I now ALWAYS have a notebook on me, it taught me something much more important. The value of receiving meaningful feedback. Feedback that directly addresses behaviors.

He was direct, but he didn't attack me as a person, he just pointed out a behavior that would help me improve in the future. He identified a mistake that I wasn't aware of.

You don't know what you don't know.

The best part? The next time I walked into a meeting with Rob, that same sales manager, he stopped and said to me "I really like your new notebook Brent, I know you'll take great notes". It felt great! True recognition – over a simple behavior change. I felt appreciated and valued.

What Rob ensured was that he followed up on his feedback, his coaching – to catch me doing it right, and provided me with Praise.

3Ps of Coaching - Preparation, Presenting, Praise

Coaching is one of those things that has many different approaches, applications, required aptitudes, and aspirations.

Given the abundance of books, videos, and courses on the subject, coaching might appear highly complex and difficult. 'Cause it is!

Here's the first problem – defining what is 'COACHING'. The reality is there are dozens and dozens of different types of coaching. Here's just a small sample:

- Professional 'coaches' who have studied for years for their certification and then sell their skills as 'life coaches' or 'executive coaches'
- Personal 'coaches' like therapists
- Fitness 'coaches'
- Sports 'coaches'
- Job performance 'coaches'

I could keep going, but you get the point!

In addition, there are all types of 'coaching' that we will have to perform in our role as a supervisor or manager supporting teams of employees.

- Coaching during interviews to help an interviewee understand why they would want to work for the company
- Coaching during employee onboarding to a new team, including the initial setting of expectations
- Coaching during training new tasks/roles
- Coaching to improve on-the-job performance
- Coaching during quarterly/annual performance evaluations
- Coaching during corrective action performance improvement plans

- Coaching to correct personality issues in the workplace
- Coaching to mentor a coworker or employee not part of your team

Again – I could keep trying to add to this list, but you get the point – there isn't just one TYPE of coaching even within the role as someone's boss.

As you expand your role within a business, you'll likely also realize that conversations with customers are 'coaching' conversations as well! Coaching customers during sales and marketing efforts to help them understand how your product or services solve a problem for them. Coaching customers while providing support, to help increase their perceived value of your product.

All that said, I think I've come up with a useful definition that covers all of these different types of coaching and different situations in which we coach:

COACHING – to inform, influence and inspire the behaviour of other people toward the progressive realization of a worthy ideal

Let me repeat that one more time – all types of coaching can be defined as 'informing, influencing and inspiring the behaviour of other people toward the progressive realization of a worthy ideal. FYI, I'm stealing a bit of a quote from Earl Nightingale here. In his famous speech titled "The Strangest Secret", Earl defines 'success' as the "progressive realization of a worthy ideal" So yeah, coaching is helping other people achieve their unique vision of success!

Now, if I were to try to write a book about every one of these different types of coaching, and all the different situations of coaching, you'd be reading an extremely long book. Each of these different situations has uniquely different appropriate coaching frameworks. So, I'm not going to do that – I'm going to focus this book on ONE type of coaching, 1-on-1 Performance Coaching. It's the type of coaching of the many different coaching actions that if done well, done consistently, done persistently, will have the greatest impact on your success in leadership.

The 3Ps of Coaching – PREPARE, PRESENT & PRAISE are the foundational skills that will apply to EVERY type of coaching. As you develop these skills, you will find ways to apply them in different coaching situations. But as I said, this book is not going to attempt to teach every coaching situation.

That said, this is a good time to define the types of behaviour categories that as a boss, you will absolutely need to identify and communicate with employees about through coaching or correction conversations.

There are 3 primary categories of behaviours that we will have conversations with employees about as a supervisor or manager – Prohibited, Personality, and Performance. Each requires different methods on exactly how we have those conversations. While this book is primarily focused on Performance, it is still important to be able to identify the differences between these types of behaviors and how to address each of them the right way.

PROHIBITED Behaviours

In my career working within a large contact center organization of 35,000 employees, directly managing teams as large as 4000 employees I've had to address all types of behaviours. Included in the things I've had to deal with are insulting or swearing at customers, theft, fraud, threatening co-workers, physical violence in the workplace and sexual harassment. These types of behaviours are non-negotiable, zero-tolerance, illegal behaviours. When this type of behaviour happens, it really isn't a conversation I would refer to as coaching, or even a Correction Conversation, that we will discuss in **Chapter 8**. Most of these types of situations result in immediate removal and termination of employment after consultation with HR. Please refer to Chapter 8 where we address this and other Correction Conversations, but bottom line, I strongly recommend NOT dealing with these on your own. Immediately consult with your boss and/or your Human Resources professional to ensure this is addressed immediately and correctly.

PERSONALITY Behaviours

Personality behaviours are the types of behaviours that may appear frequently. Behaviours like absenteeism, tardiness, using their personal phone or checking social media when they should be working, dressing unprofessionally/incorrectly for the workplace, or interpersonal communication/relationship issues with co-workers. In most cases, the type of coaching for these types of issues is a straightforward conversation to reset expectations of what is acceptable in your workplace in alignment with your company values and role expectations. Again, these types of behaviors may be common, yet they are essential to be addressed as early as possible. As a mentor of mine, Dr. Harvey Silver commonly stated, "problem behaviour ignored is problem behavior encouraged". We will address these types of 'Correction Conversations' in **Chapter 8**.

PERFORMANCE Behaviours

Ok, now we're getting to the good stuff. Where you really get to shine as a good boss! Dealing with both prohibited and personality behaviors correctly is a necessary and essential part of being a good boss. But where you can truly stand out, be celebrated for your skills as a leader and make meaningful connections with people is how you handle coaching on-the-job performance behaviours. Yet, even within coaching performance behaviours there is a layer of complexity to how you will coach – due to something I refer to SKILL vs WILL.

'Skill' is the capacity for someone's ability to do the job. 'Will' is the willingness to do it. When you have team members with high skill and high will, it makes your job easy! However, as you are likely aware, like all things, people will fall somewhere on a spectrum between low and high skill AND low and high will. Being able to identify SKILL vs WILL and knowing how to handle them differently is where the skill of being a good boss comes in.

Essentially there are going to be 4 types of employees as it relates to performance behaviour:

HIGH SKILL/HIGH WILL – We like these people! Praise them, but don't neglect them. Regardless of how good someone is, they can keep improving. Even Lebron James, Tiger Woods and Lionel Messi have coaches that evaluate their performance and give them regular coaching. These are also folks who can help teach you new and better ways to improve!

HIGH SKILL/LOW WILL – These types of employees are very capable of doing the job, they just aren't motivated to do it. They will need coaching! But if it persists and doesn't improve, this coaching can quickly turn to a correction conversation, moved to a different role or even removed from the business.

LOW SKILL/HIGH WILL – These employees are more than willing to do a good job, they are either lacking the knowledge/experience or capacity to do the job. Often, these may be newer employees still learning the ropes, or employees that may be in the wrong job based on their natural abilities.

LOW SKILL/LOW WILL – These are the folks who aren't motivated nor capable of doing the job. Likely they need to be moved either to a new role or out of the company.

To better identify if you should be addressing PERFORMANCE BEHAVIOURS through regular 1:1 Performance Coaching or Correction Conversations, take a look at the matrix in the image below:

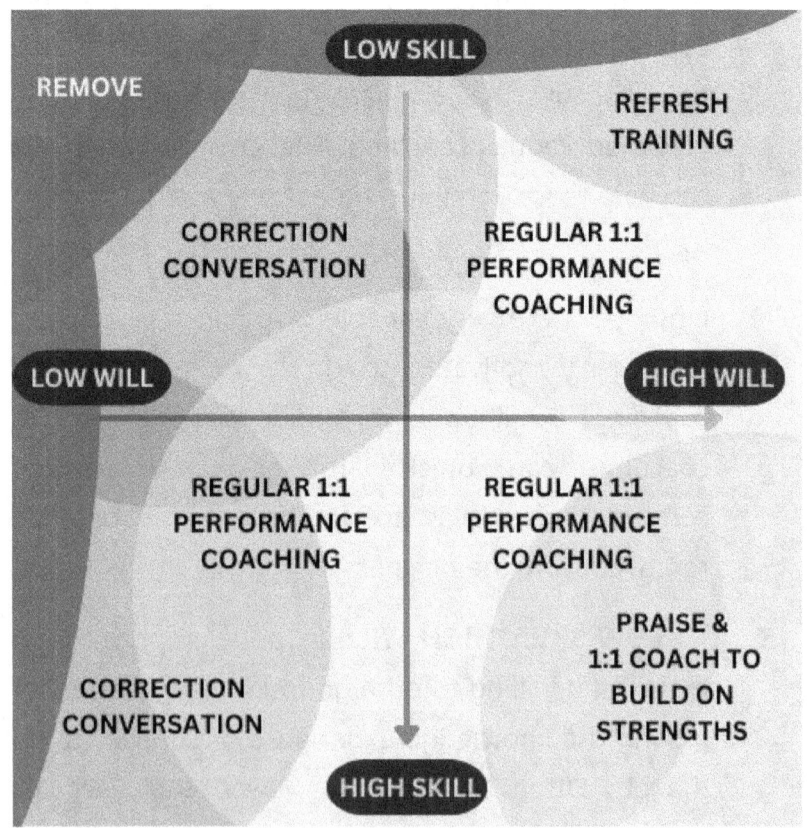

As you can see, most employees will benefit from 1-to-1 Recurring Job Performance coaching. My best advice is if you think it's time for a Correction Conversation, you should consult with your manager to get their help. Again, if it's time for a Correction Conversation, flip to Chapter 8 on properly handling these types of conversations.

For the other chapters in the book, I'm going to focus specifically on **1-to-1 RECURRING JOB PERFORMANCE** coaching. This is the type of coaching that you will need to use the most *frequently* and which has the greatest *impact* on your success in your role as someone's boss.

This is the coaching we will discuss. I've personally coached thousands of employees, I've evaluated and trained the coaching activities of thousands of managers and supervisors, and I've seen first-hand what coaching has worked best to build a successful business that directly generated almost $1B of revenue. Regular 1-on-1 recurring job performance coaching is the single most important leadership and management activity a good boss applies to support their team.

Let's dive in.

Can I coach?

Are you capable of giving praise? If not, stop now…you won't be able to coach!

Can you speak with confidence about the things you know and observe? No? You are going to have difficulty coaching...coaches need to be confident and effective communicators to present well, no mumbling your words!

Do you know how to competently do the task/job of the person being coached? It's OK if you can't do it better than them, but you need to have actual experience to demonstrate an effective understanding of the task you are coaching to prepare to coach.

If you are: Capable of doing the job to PREPARE; able to PRESENT with Confidence; and willing to give PRAISE; then we can make you an awesome coach.

Chapter 4:
1st P of COACHING – PREPARE

Before you start coaching, you need to have clarity of the purpose (WHY) and result (WHAT) of the coaching you're about to do:

- PURPOSE of Coaching (WHY) - Strengthen the 3Ps of the Business

  o PEOPLE - the person you're coaching grows, improves, and benefits from doing their job better

  o PRODUCT - the quality of the output of the work improves, improving the quality of the product or service for the customer

  o PROFIT - happy customers buy more products, the business makes more money - or perhaps your coaching simply helps the person work smarter & faster which also improves profitability for the business

- Desired RESULT (What) of Coaching

  o Create an opportunity to provide PRAISE for the person being coached

Now that you know why you're coaching, and what the outcome of coaching should be, we can move on to actually PREPARE to coach!!

3Ps of PREPARE – PROFILE, PREVIEW, PROBE

1ˢᵗ P of Preparing – PROFILE – What do you know about the person you are coaching?

I like to keep all the pertinent facts I know about a person in one place, the same place I document their coaching. As most people will likely be using this information in the context of coaching an employee, I'll use a boss/employee framework for illustration - but yes, this can apply to nearly all other coaching relationships!

Whenever I had someone new join my team, of course if I had interviewed them, I would have had my notes from the interview about their story. Often, I would have people join my team who were transferred from other teams, or in many cases I inherited new teams of people. Regardless of how someone became part of my team, the very first thing I'd get them to do would be to share with me their story. I'd usually say something like "OK, so starting from kindergarten, tell me how we got here!" Listening intently, I'd take good notes, carefully listening to what was truly important to them, and along the way, of course, I'd capture essential pieces of information that help me understand their unique *profile* as a person.

In addition to the unique parts of their story that told me what's truly important to them, some of those essential elements I'd want to be listening for:

- Proper spelling of the name they use, including how to *pronounce* it correctly

- Who are the other people in their life that will benefit from their success at work that they want to share

- Approximate age

- When did they start working for the company?

- Where did they work before, what previous careers, and for how long?

- What level of education & field of study?

- Current Salary & date of their last raise

- Significant hobbies/outside interests

Now you're already saying, "Wait a second, I only have 8 people reporting to me that I need to coach, why do I need to write all this down, I can remember that much about the people on my team".

And you're right, likely you can, however, if you're any good at coaching, you are going to lose team members because they get promoted, or maybe you'll get transferred to another department in 6 months. No matter how good of a boss you are, you'll have team members leave and new ones join....pretty soon those 8 people you have on your team will be 25 different folks that come and go and you never know when they may end up back on your team. Or maybe you get promoted and those 8 people are part of a larger team of 50 people, why risk losing everything you know about these people you worked so hard to develop great relationships with?

Or maybe you're saying, "Hey man, we shouldn't reduce people down to demographics".

Again, you're right! But this does matter – it matters to THEM! I'm not recommending we coach people *differently* based on these demographics, yet remembering important things about what makes them unique, what's important to them, is important! I'll say this again, understanding this information is NOT about labeling people and should NEVER be used in any way that would conflict with being inclusive in our approach to coaching. It's meant to ensure we demonstrate we care about their story. But we only capture what personal information they WANT to share, what's important to them!!

Bottom line - best to have it written down, and accessible when you need it (especially when preparing for coaching) versus not be able to remember it!

What are their goals?

Remember, the coaching isn't for you, it's for them…so you better know what THEY want. It's going to be pointless to coach someone who doesn't want to improve or achieve something specific. If you aren't clear about what desired results they want, any coaching you provide will go in one ear and out the other. You can influence but ultimately any coaching will have to be aligned with THEIR goals, not yours.

Knowing the goals of the people you are going to coach is essential. If you haven't asked them, don't guess, just ask them!

- What are they trying to accomplish with their job in the next 3 months, 12 months, or 3 years?

- Is this a career or just a side gig on their way to something completely different?

- Do they have specific financial rewards they want to achieve for themselves?

Understanding their story and their goals helps you build a PROFILE to understand how to prepare for coaching for THEM for the results that are meaningful for THEM.

2nd P of Preparing – PREVIEW

If you coached them previously, what was it you coached?

Important!! If you coached them previously it better be documented....no documentation means you have nothing to follow up on, which means you may have wasted your time and theirs.

To repeat, documenting is key. Maybe you have 12 people on your team to whom you give regular coaching...if you don't document it, you can't expect yourself to remember the specific behaviours you worked on last time, let alone just remember what the KPI/desired result of coaching was for every person on your team.

Heck, even if you only have 2 people you give coaching to, do yourself a favor and DOCUMENT your coaching!

Before going any further preparing for coaching, read your notes from the last coaching session. Remind yourself of what you coached previously so you can ensure those behaviours have improved and make sure you don't repeat yourself needlessly.

Have some way to take notes. No notes, no coaching! When preparing for coaching, review what you've coached before.

What is their past performance?

Are there reports, or metrics to review?

Importantly, what has been the trend of their results - have they been improving, declining, or flat-lining?

This analysis of past performance is going to be dependent on the type of work being evaluated and coached...but ultimately, every job has specific KPIs (key performance indicators) that can be used to determine if someone is meeting targets, improving in their job, or getting worse. If you don't have agreed-upon KPIs that will be used to evaluate the results of someone's job performance, then it will be difficult to hold them accountable or even more importantly reward them for a job well done.

It doesn't matter if someone is a janitor, a burger flipper, a lawyer, or a pilot - every job has an opportunity to create and measure KPIs. If you recall from the 3Ps of Management – Planning, Processes and Performance – you need the right measurements of performance to help evaluate what processes are working to achieve those plans.

However, I've found that picking the RIGHT KPIs and then communicating the expectations and properly measuring them is one of the largest failures in many organization, specifically as it relates to individual job performance.

One of the best examples of organizations with a strong KPI culture is professional sports...stats, stats, and more stats. It's rarely in doubt when one player is performing well or lagging behind - the stats are clearly communicated, everyone knows the expectations, and the players are the first ones to know when they are missing their KPIs. Most organizations can learn a lot from how to measure and reward employees from the examples set by pro sports.

What makes a good KPI?

- Aligned with impacts on the 3Ps of Business – PEOPLE, PRODUCT, PROFIT

- Reflective of short-term performance against a measure of time (per Minute, Hour, Day, etc.) or as a percentage/ratio of two important measurements of their work

- Capable of being relatively measured against peers AND their own historical performance

- Have at least one EFFICIENCY KPI (quantitative – how fast, or how many) and one EFFECTIVENESS KPI (qualitative – how well, measurable value) for any specific job or role

E.g. - The Shoe Salesman

The simplest measure for salespeople is often TOTAL SALES REVENUE over a period of time (week or month). Assuming all the salespeople in that store work an equal number of hours in that same timeframe, then yes, this is an effective way to measure performance. However, in retail sales, the number of hours worked by individual employees can often vary, meaning a better 'efficiency' KPI could be TOTAL SALES $/HOURS WORKED.

One KPI likely isn't enough to help coach a salesman though. At a minimum, in addition to Sales$/hour, you would also want to know their #Sales/Hour (a secondary efficiency KPI) and Average Sales Amount (an effectiveness KPI).

Different KPIs reflect different areas of opportunity as it relates to BEHAVIOURS...remember, when coaching you should not, in fact, you cannot coach results, you can only coach BEHAVIOURS, which means getting a trending view of the RIGHT KPIs can give you insight into behaviours.

Let's look at an example to illustrate what I mean...

$ Sales/Hr	Last Week	Week Prior	2 Weeks Ago	3 Weeks Ago	4 Weeks Ago	5 Weeks Ago
Blake	$100	$111	$116	$111	$99	$93
Steve	$100	$111	$116	$111	$99	$93

Blake and Steve have IDENTICAL Sales $/hour performance over the past 6 weeks and both slipped this past week vs their previous high week. If we only looked at that ONE metric, we'd think we could coach them essentially the same. However, if we look at one layer below, we see a much different picture:

Average Sale Amount	Last Week	Week Prior	2 Weeks Ago	3 Weeks Ago	4 Weeks Ago	5 Weeks Ago
Blake	$50	$53	$55	$53	$52	$49
Steve	$75	$78	$80	$80	$76	$72
# Sales/Hr						
Blake	2.0	2.1	2.1	2.1	1.9	1.9
Steve	1.3	1.4	1.5	1.4	1.3	1.3

Now with a bit more insight, we see that while Blake sells way more shoes, he sells significantly less expensive items than Steve. The net results for each are the same, however, looking at it this way demonstrates that they go about getting those results much differently from one another.

Do you still think we should coach them the same?

Obviously, they have different sales BEHAVIOURS that are creating these different results...if somehow you could combine their best qualities, Blake's ability to sell a lot of shoes and Steve's ability to sell higher value products, instead of averaging $105/hour, they could have averaged $153!

In other words, when we coach Blake, we should be looking for behaviours to help him sell higher-value products and when coaching Steve, we should focus on behaviours to help him close MORE actual sales.

Just as important to paying attention to the RIGHT KPI to help you identify potentially results-impacting behaviours is paying attention to TRENDS. This is especially important when doing recurring coaching, as it can help you identify if previous coaching is making a difference in results. It also is important - especially if you have multiple metrics that determine different types of results (efficiency vs effectiveness). If one of the metrics has been showing consistent improvement over time it likely makes sense to focus on the metric that has stalled or moved in the wrong direction. With a metric moving in the right direction, it implies the person already is aware of how to improve as they are making progress without your coaching - help them where they most need the help!

Sahar's Performance	Last Week	Week Prior	2 Weeks Ago	3 Weeks Ago	4 Weeks Ago	5 Weeks Ago
Customer Satisfaction	75%	80%	85%	84%	88%	90%
$ Sales/Hour	$100	$95	$92	$88	$82	$75

In the example above, even if $100/hour is not near the target of $150/HR, I'd want to focus my coaching attention on customer satisfaction behaviours vs sales tactics - Sahar has been steadily improving her sales without any coaching but seems something has been starting to piss potential customers off.

Perhaps you think, "She's sucking at both sales and customer satisfaction…I need to coach both!" Wrong! You can't fix everything all at once…if you want to coach effectively, you need to ensure FOCUS. Pick the ONE result you want to impact with your coaching today, not only will it allow you to concentrate your evaluation on specific behaviours related to that one result, but it will also give you a much more likely chance that your coaching will work. If you try to improve multiple results and then multiple behaviours, you'll end up coaching nothing in the end. Focus and coach to one desired result - the one that will create the largest benefit, then move on to the next in a future coaching opportunity. Choose a 'POINT OF FOCUS'.

The importance of choosing a point of focus and coaching behaviors, not results is something that was reinforced for me by Sprint's former SVP Customer Care, Marci Carris. Sprint, which merged with T-Mobile in 2021, was one of the world's largest corporations and the 3rd largest mobile phone provider in the USA, with over 50 million customers. In her role as SVP Customer Care, Marci was responsible for every single customer interaction with every Sprint customer that occurred outside a retail store. In total, Marci was responsible for the conversations that over 25,000 customer service associates had with Sprint customers every day. When I asked Marci about the most important factor when coaching those associates, here's what she shared with me. "You need to pick ONE primary AREA OF FOCUS. Work with your associate on that one issue by evaluating them doing the job, and work on behaviors related to that area of focus. Don't disregard the other issues completely but put them aside until the associate makes progress on the area of focus, then move to the next area for improvement. Inspect what you expect. Identify behaviors not outcomes."

Great, now you've reviewed their PROFILE:

- Know who you're coaching
- Know what their goals are

And you've PREVIEWED:

- Know what you coached previously
- Know how they've been performing recently against the KPIs important for them
- Know what FOCUS POINT (KPI) you are going to impact with your coaching

Like EVERY part of this coaching system, preparing for coaching is a SKILL - the more you do it, the more feedback you get about it, the better you get at it.

Next step - PROBE!

3rd P of Preparing – PROBE

If you really know your stuff, that is, you know how to do the task you're coaching, then it will make probing, by evaluating their actual work much easier. If you don't, you are going to be in trouble. It's difficult to evaluate something you don't know much about. Remember, one of the first requirements of coaching - you need to know how to do the thing you're going to coach.

I'm going to assume you aren't going to try to coach people about things you don't know enough about to help them improve. Again, you don't actually have to be better at it than them, I'm sure Messi is a better soccer player than his coach, but I bet his coach knows quite a bit about soccer.

You will need to base your coaching on a PROBE of their current capabilities – an evaluation. You can do an evaluation live – watching them do the task, or if it's available use a recording or a review of work already completed.

Check yourself - you're not going to evaluate everything - remember in the PREVIEW step you identified a FOCUS POINT for this coaching. If you're coaching a barista at Starbucks and you are trying to help them make a Chai Tea Latte faster, don't worry about identifying behaviours related to how they smile and greet the customers.

While evaluating you should make notes...regardless of what is being evaluated...think of a +/- or pros/cons list with a twist...keeping the FOCUS POINT in mind, make note of their GOOD behaviours that are helping them related to your chosen focus point (CONTINUE), what are their BAD behaviours which are hurting their performance relative to that focus point (STOP) and what are their MISSING behaviours that could help them be better in the future (START).

If you happen to be evaluating someone regarding a routine task they complete dozens of times a day, for example, a customer service interaction, perhaps you're asking "why not use a quality checklist"?

Short answer - you're their coach, not a Quality Inspector - we're not trying to probe to evaluate the entire task or everything they do - we want to identify specific behaviours related to the FOCUS POINT we determined we need to target if we're going to help this unique individual achieve their goals. I'm not saying a QA form isn't valuable or serves its own purpose - it certainly does, but if we want to be a good coach, we won't need to complete an entire checklist to identify the most impactful behaviours as it relates to the point of focus of our coaching. We need to focus on the behaviors that will help them improve the most.

I'm going to share with you my 'ULTIMATE 3P EVALUATION FORM' you can use to evaluate while you're probing to prepare for your next coaching session.

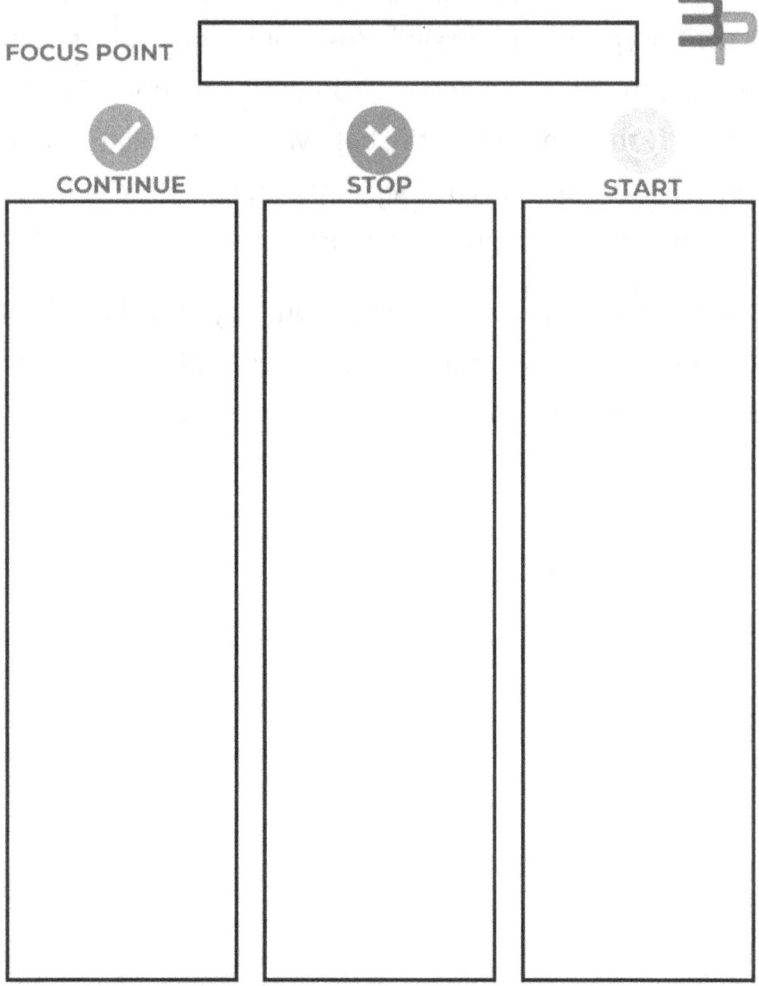

Pretty straightforward, right? The problem with a traditional checklist, it's trying to evaluate EVERYTHING. If we prepared well for our coaching and identified the right focus point in our PREVIEW, we are evaluating with that focus in mind. A full checklist won't create focus. That said, if completing a full-checklist is part of YOUR job expectations, you can fill it out, and then use the

CONTINUE/STOP/START evaluation form to guide your coaching.

LIVE Evaluation

Often, we can't remotely observe or have a recording to use for the evaluation of a task - we need to evaluate it as it happens. Here's a vital piece of advice - DON'T correct or give live feedback - keep your thoughts to yourself and your Continue/Stop/Start list. This is hard! If they stop to ask questions, go ahead and provide support, maybe add to your notes, but don't VOLUNTEER feedback while evaluating. Keep your mouth shut. Remember they likely have been doing this task dozens if not hundreds of times without you watching over their shoulder - and will continue to make those mistakes unless you give them great coaching. Great coaching is dependent on a great evaluation - which means an uninterrupted evaluation of their abilities. If they break something that needs correcting, let them break it and then go back and fix it later (unless it's a zero-tolerance, prohibited behaviour).

Remember the FOCUS POINT you are trying to impact - again, you may observe some great or terrible behaviours, but unless those behaviours impact the desired result of this coaching session - it's OK and in fact, better if you ignore behaviours not related to the FOCUS POINT for now. You want your evaluation to stay focused - if you're coaching something to help their efficiency - how quickly something needs to get done - then you have to ignore some behaviours that should and could be improved relating to their effectiveness - or the quality of the task. Remember, you'll have another coaching session in the future but today you already decided you need to help them improve their efficiency!

💡 Note - if you do observe a deal-breaking, zero-tolerance, PROHIBITED behaviour, something that is breaking the rules or demonstrating a lack of integrity, don't ignore it! But you also shouldn't make it part of the coaching session. If you identify behaviours like this - STOP what you're doing and deal with them as a CORRECTION CONVERSATION based on the severity of the issue. We don't coach integrity issues or concerns - we need to have zero-tolerance for PROHIBITED behaviors like cheating/lying/stealing - those are integrity issues. See Chapter 8 on having good CORRECTION CONVERSATIONS.

BE SPECIFIC – IDENTIFY BEHAVIOURS NOT RESULTS

You are trying to identify BEHAVIOURS...behaviours are things people SAY or DO...behaviours are what drive the results. Results are outcomes...you can't coach results, only behaviours.

Eg. Instead of "stop making customers angry" (result) vs identifying specifically what they say that makes customers angry - "stop making fun of customers' hometown when greeting them." (behaviour).

I'm going to belabour this point. This is, without a doubt, the biggest mistake hopeful coaches make when evaluating and coaching someone they're trying to help. They go on to provide coaching based on getting a better result without identifying root cause behaviours. This is why many people hate getting coached - telling someone what result you would like to improve without discussing the behaviour change necessary to impact results is frustrating as hell. If they already knew how to improve the result, they would have done so on their own...telling someone what results you want, without helping them on the HOW TO, is a quick way to piss people off. Imagine if Lebron James' coach just kept telling him he needed to score more points during the game.

BE SPECIFIC is also key here - you need to be able to reference exactly what the desired behaviour change is. When does it occur? When it occurs, does something happen immediately preceding the bad habit? This way, they can identify unwanted behaviour before it happens in the future. More specific = easier to coach. If you only identify vague behaviours, then don't expect positive results from your coaching.

Ultimately you want to end up with 3 lists from your notes

1. Behaviours to CONTINUE (good habits)
2. Behaviours to STOP (bad habits)
3. Behaviours to START (missing good habits)

- - Note - to identify missing habits, you may need to observe the task being coached from start to finish. You may need to make this list only AFTER you observed the action you want to coach - but these are things you need to ensure you identify as they are the most impactful aspect of the coaching you will deliver - these are the missing good habits that the person you're coaching likely isn't even aware of which can help them improve. They don't know what they don't know!

Next, prioritize the list! You can't coach EVERYTHING you observed. Go through your lists of 'continue', 'stop', 'start' behaviors and circle or highlight the MOST important behaviours that will have the most significant impact on the desired result - remember to align with the Focus Point you chose before you started evaluating!

- Of the behaviours you want to CONTINUE...pick one, the best one...ignore the rest (but save your notes for next time to compare and build upon in a future coaching session).

- Of the bad habits, pick ONE and only one...the worst one, the biggest thing messing up potential success as it relates to the result/KPI/FOCUS POINT you chose for this coaching session

- Of the missing good habits ...pick ONE and make sure it's one you know how to do well....because you're going to need to demonstrate/role play this. They likely don't know how/when/why to do this thing or else they'd already be doing it!!!

Now your previously messy notes should look something like this but with better handwriting than mine! (Ideally, you would be documenting this using a tool to document all your coaching, even if just a spreadsheet!).

CONTINUE

Recapping the 3 key points of your presentation within your conclusion!

STOP

Reading the words directly from the presentation slides like you did when you reviewed slide 5.

START

Add visual images to replace text-heavy content (eg. slide 6) to allow yourself to speak naturally

This summarized CONTINUE, STOP, START list – the result of your PROBING by evaluation is going to be the foundation and core of your actual coaching session. This is what you will discuss and what you will share after you finish your feedback conversation.

Next chapter - PRESENT!

Chapter 5:
PRESENT

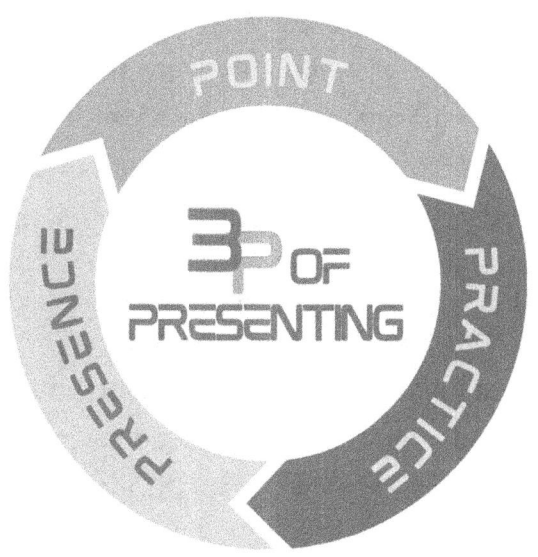

Presentation is the delivery part of the 'art of communication'. Being a good boss is directly dependent on your ability to be good at communicating with others. Becoming great at communication is something people continually learn to improve upon over their entire lifetime.

Great presentation skills are another subject we could spend countless hours discussing. One of my favorite quotes on the subject comes from perhaps the world's most famous investor, Warren Buffet. While addressing a group of business students he said "Right now, I would pay $100,000 for 10 percent of the future earnings of any of you, so if you're interested, see me after class. Now, you can improve your value by 50 percent just by learning communication skills--public speaking. If that's the case, see me after class and I'll pay you $150,000."

This quote may actually understate the value of being good at communicating, regardless, without a doubt, presenting is one of the foundational skills of supporting a successful business and being successful ourselves.

Again, this book is not going to try to teach you how to be a great communicator or presenter in all situations. We're going to focus on the most frequent, and as a result, the most immediately important situation where you'll need to communicate with employees. During regular, 1-on-1 performance coaching sessions.

In the last chapter, we covered what was needed to properly prepare for our coaching session. We refreshed our understanding of the persons' PROFILE, determined a desired result for the coaching session then we identified a FOCUS POINT by PREVIEWING past performance and we've PROBED current performance with a great evaluation. We have a clear summary of what they should CONTINUE, STOP and START doing to best improve their performance related to the desired result. Now we need to have a conversation...and we better get it right. Poorly presented coaching - even with the best intentions and planning, or the highest quality insightful evaluation - can result in exactly the opposite results if we don't know how to PRESENT the feedback well.

1st P of Presenting – POINT

Now is a good time to remind yourself of the fundamental WHY & WHAT of your coaching in the first place. Remember WHY we're coaching in the first place - to help them grow and improve relative to the 3Ps of businesses (People, Product & Profit) - and WHAT - to create an opportunity to give them PRAISE! If you deliver coaching with the right purpose in mind, and an understanding of

WHY & WHAT you intended to coach, you'll be less likely to mess up your feedback. Start with the WHY & WHAT. You want to help them be successful so you can catch them doing it right so you can give them Praise to make them feel appreciated!

Can't I just send them my notes? No! They need COACHING, an opportunity to clarify, discuss, and create a dialogue with you. As a reminder, if you identified a ***major*** behavioural issue that was cause for significant concern, it is NOT appropriate to discuss it in a coaching feedback session. ALWAYS keep CORRECTION CONVERSATIONS separate from coaching feedback sessions (see Chapter 8). I'll repeat, I'm not saying delay that conversation – it should happen ASAP, before, but not during the coaching session!

So, what do I mean by ensuring to have a POINT to your presenting of feedback?

Before you begin presenting your coaching, have a clear vision of the **desired result** of the coaching. Refresh what the FOCUS POINT of your evaluation you completed during the PREPARE stage, refresh what the most important behaviours you want to help them CONTINUE, STOP and START. If they use this coaching, how will it help them GROW and IMPROVE? What potential impact will it have on their performance? Refresh yourself on WIIFT – What's In It For Them – if they apply this coaching. This is the point of the coaching you're about to PRESENT. Keep the point in mind during your entire coaching conversation.

Your POINT should come across in how you begin your coaching, be supported by the evidence of what you want them to CONTINUE, STOP & START doing, and how you wrap up the coaching by incorporating what's in it for them (WIIFT) and summarizing the coaching.

2nd P of Presenting – PRACTICE

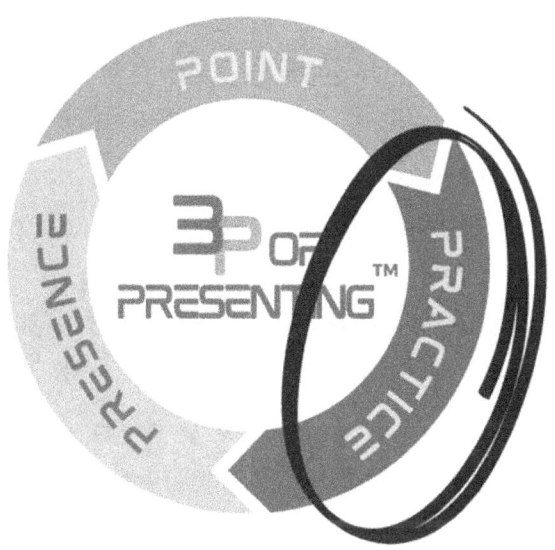

As with any skill, in any area of your life, you improve through PRACTICE. You inherently know this. This is NOT new information! And without a doubt, PRESENTING, including presenting coaching is a SKILL. After working with thousands of people, I can confidently say that the ability to communicate – to present – is the single most important skill anyone in a leadership and management role develops.

PRACTICE makes perfect, right? Nope – no such thing as perfect. In my three decades in the customer service industry, I've handled or listened to over 100,000 customer service phone calls, but never heard a perfect one. I've participated in or evaluated 10's of thousands of coaching sessions but never witnessed a perfect one. Practice doesn't make perfect, but it will help make the skills required to present effectively better. I much prefer the saying 'practice makes permanent'. Practice helps create habits.

You can practice presenting your coaching in several ways. If you're not quite ready to deliver it to an employee on your team, you can practice what you're planning to say in front of a mirror. Another way could be to practice by recording yourself on camera, watching it back, and evaluating yourself. If you have a trusted co-worker, you could role-play with them and get their feedback on how you did. Likely the best way to practice, however, is to practice with your boss and get their feedback!

The most valuable way to practice and improve is being evaluated by others. Remember, experience is not the best teacher, evaluated experience is. I strongly recommend asking your boss to regularly evaluate how you are delivering coaching sessions with your team members.

First, have your boss review the coaching notes you created to prepare for a coaching session.

- Did you review their PROFILE to capture what might be important to them? Did you correctly identify WIIFT (What's-In-It-For-Them) to grow and improve related to their goals?
- Did you correctly identify the right FOCUS POINT from the PREVIEW stage when you reviewed their past performance?
- Did you identify the most impactful behaviours to continue, stop, start when you PROBED by evaluating their work?

Next, have your boss silently observe you deliver coaching to an employee. Effectively, have them probe, by evaluating you delivering coaching! Have them identify YOUR behaviors that you should CONTINUE, STOP and START doing when delivering coaching!

Bottom line, just like your employees who will always be able to grow and improve, regardless how good they are, you will always be able to improve how you deliver coaching. I've been presenting coaching for decades, and I continue to practice, I continue to get feedback, I continue to learn and innovate how I coach. Practice does not make perfect – when it comes to conversations, our ability to present - there is no such thing! But it sure as hell keeps us improving!

3rd P of Presenting – PRESENCE

Presenting with *presence* is about how you say the words vs the content of your words. Presence during any type of presentation includes things like:

- Clarity – ensuring the words being used are understandable by the person you are presenting to
- Eye contact – looking at the person you're speaking to
- Facial expressions – ensuring your facial expression matches what you're saying
- Body language – posture, what you do with your hands to help illustrate what you're saying and that you're confident and comfortable speaking

- Tone of Voice – your tone of voice should also match the content. Things like your pitch (high pitch/low pitch), pace
- Vocal Variety – that you mix up the tone of voice throughout to align with what you're saying and avoid coming across monotone
- Awareness of your audience – adjusting all of the above to create better engagement with the person/people you are presenting to by reading their body language

You may be thinking, "wait a second, these sound like skills for public speaking"? And you'd be right, they are! However, in 1-on-1 coaching sessions, all of these things are vitally important to deliver – to *present* – effective coaching.

In a 1-on-1 situation, the most important action to demonstrate PRESENCE while presenting is **proactive listening.** A 1-on-1 regular performance coaching session is a dialogue. It's not you on stage delivering coaching! It's about ensuring that you have identified behaviours they can and want to improve upon. That what you thought was important to them actually is! That they understand how modifying the behaviours you identified can and will help them.

The entire time you are delivering (presenting) your coaching, you will need to be LISTENING as well. That you are reading and adjusting to *their* eye contact, body language, and tone of voice! If they have different goals than you previously understood, you adjust and update your *profile* of them.

I'm going to repeat this point – presenting with PRESENCE is about being PRESENT – that we demonstrate our presence, especially in a 1:1 coaching situation through our ability to be present in the conversation and listen well.

Presenting with Presence is a skill, that you can and will improve upon, the more you practice!

All 3P's of PRESENTING - PUTTING IT TOGETHER

Here are the key steps to PRESENTING coaching feedback during 1-on-1 regular performance coaching sessions...ensure you have reviewed your notes to remind you of the point, practiced, and present with PRESENCE:

1. SMILE

• Start a conversation with them light and friendly - please make sure you are SMILING! Let them know what you have reviewed, that you have evaluated their efforts, that you have some ideas about behaviours to help them improve, and what impact successful coaching will have on their results. * TIP* Best to make sure they have a way to take notes if possible, and if not, that you have a way to send your coaching summary to them! Because you took notes and created a summary of the coaching, right?

2. POINT

- Introduce the POINT of this coaching - how it will improve their performance results and how that performance will help them achieve their personal goals.

3. CONTINUE

- Next, discuss the one behaviour they should continue - be specific, remember, you must specify the actual thing they said or did, not the result of what they said or did

Eg. "I liked how your follow-through on your swing stayed in a straight line from the contact with the ball", not "I liked your follow-through"

- Remember, this is a DIALOGUE, ensure they know what you're talking about and they agree!

4. STOP

- Discuss the ONE behaviour to STOP and WHY it's hurting their performance!! Again, the more specific you can be the better. When did they do this, what preceded its occurrence, and how can they identify ways to stop it before it happens in the future? Remember to relate to them why this behaviour is negatively impacting their performance vs the FOCUS POINT/desired result. Ask questions and LISTEN to make sure they actually know what the heck you're talking about. We should try to get to the root cause of this behavior. WHY are they doing it. Like a kid, we should ask 'why' 3 times. They are the ones doing it, but unless we get to the root cause, it will be difficult to change this behavior. Maybe they were trained incorrectly. Perhaps their incentives aren't aligned or their understanding of the incentives aren't aligned. But only through asking why, and LISTENING, will we be able to influence the desired behavior change.

5. START

- Next, it's time to discuss the ONE behaviour to START...this should be a two-way conversation as you are going to have to instruct, influence, demonstrate, **role-play**, and practice this new behavior. They are going to need to show you they understand what you are trying to tell them to start doing. But more importantly you should let the show you what they're capable of! This is an opportunity for them to be creative. Let them figure it out!

Have them create a new behavior based on your influence and inspiration but let them shine. You should ensure you reinforce why they should start doing this thing, how it will improve results, and make them more awesome - but through the role play, they should make it their OWN.. Repeat and repeat the role play as many times as necessary (if you have to do it 10 times then you have to do it 10 times) until they can demonstrate they can turn this new skill you are guiding them towards into a repeatable behaviour. Please refer to the text box at the end of this chapter detailing how to complete effective roleplay.

6. WIIFT

· Now it's time to discuss "What's In It For Them" (WIIFT) if they heed your coaching efforts. (some of you may have heard this represented as WIFFM – or "what's in it for 'ME'" – but since this book is about you providing coaching for THEM, we're going to use WIIFT!). This is not just about how applying these behaviour changes will improve their performance results, but specifically, what's in it for them if they achieve this improved performance. Ensure the WIIFT you discuss is aligned with what you knew about this person coming into the coaching session from their PROFILE - are they keen on career advancement or is money their primary drive? Are they desperately hungry for public recognition or do they take immense pleasure in personal improvement? Whatever you conclude when discussing WIIFT, make sure it's aligned with what you already knew about the person. If you didn't already know, discussing it now will certainly help you better understand what motivates them - which you can use in future coaching sessions (because you are taking detailed NOTES and you will update their PROFILE).

7. RECAP and CONFIRM

· Now it's time to RECAP and CONFIRM - encourage them to repeat back what behaviour they should Continue, the one they should Stop, and the new behaviour they are going to Start. If you have to help them during the recap, no problem - but repeat the recap until they can recall those identified behaviours without guidance. Recap the WIIFT -

again, how will this improve their performance results and specifically WIIFT - what will they get out of it if they achieve this improved performance? Now that they can demonstrate back to you what you've coached, get them to confirm they will do it the next time they perform the task you were coaching.

8. THANK THEM

- Thank them and give a reminder that you are here to support them. Tell them you appreciate spending the time talking with them. This is an underrated principle of leadership which needs to be reinforced here. Without them, your position wouldn't exist. Without them, the company wouldn't be able to provide the same quality of product to its' customers or enable the business to earn profits. A simple, but specific, thank you is an easy hack to remind someone that you value them.

I want to reinforce here that this should be a dialogue. If we were to record and measure your coaching conversation and measure what percentage of the conversation they were speaking vs you speaking that they were speaking more than you. This should not be you dictating to them. No dictating! Yes, you are giving direct feedback and you embrace providing direct feedback well. We're identifying behaviors they should stop and start doing, but we're making it about them and with them. That they are the primary focus and active participant in the conversation.

My friend and colleague, Doug Jones, former co-owner and country head for a large customer service provider stated that when having any conversation, *"Make sure your ears are bigger than your mouth"*.

Coaching for Success – A Case Study

In 2002, alongside Sue Nokes, Deborah Lewis was brought in to help drive the customer experience (CX) transformation at T-Mobile from the ground up. Sue was charged with leading the CX teams of 18,000 employees to help bring T-Mobile from the bottom of JD Power's customer satisfaction rankings. Sue entrusted Deb with leading the human resources team to instill a customer-centric culture within T-Mobile. This meant not just defining the vision and setting the values, but ensuring these elements were woven into every level with the golden thread of alignment throughout the organization, by identifying the critical behaviors required for each role and responsibility.

Over the next 18 months, through dedicated focus and strategic intervention, their team was able to propel T-Mobile to the top of the JD Power rankings, keeping them there for 11 straight cycles.

They accomplished this through a cultural transformation, embedded in the entire ecosystem of technology systems, methods and procedures, training, and coaching – all aligned with putting the customer at the heart of every role and responsibility.

After her successes at T-Mobile, Deb's next task was to help drive a similar customer-centric cultural transformation for Charter Communications. There, she again joined the executive team to instill a vision, values, and supporting training around the new Customer Experience culture that was previously lacking. Within 18 months they were able to drive a 30-point increase in the overall Net Promoter Score (a common measure of customer satisfaction) through a focused effort of supporting the field technicians. Unlike a call center, where supervisors can listen to calls or review call recordings, these technicians worked independently as they visited customer homes to repair issues.

Deb and the leadership team modified the responsibilities of the Field Supervisors and added additional field support by doing ride-alongs with their field service technicians to provide supportive feedback-based coaching fueled by observation in the field! According to Deb, "You have to know what's going on – you need to know the behavior" of the people you're going to coach. In addition, they added daily 15-minute huddles along with their weekly 1-hour team huddles with the field service techs where in both the weekly and daily huddles they focused the discussion on the customer experience through roleplaying customer interactions.

At the end of the day, Deb emphasizes that it's all about behaviors. While metrics on a scorecard are important to measure the progress of performance, change happens through coaching of behaviors. "You may have sold 10 widgets yesterday, but if we want improvement, we need to identify and coach the behaviors". To do this "I have to be able to observe what you're doing".

In the next chapter, we'll go into detail on how to properly close the loop and complete a proper follow-up to your coaching session.

** **ROLE-PLAYING** **. Being good at role-playing is a developed skill. Like all skills, it gets better with experience, specifically when you also get evaluated on that experience. Ideally, you have your own coach who can observe how you are giving coaching feedback and performing role-playing in your coaching, so you can receive their feedback about how to improve. This is key to the PRACTICE element of being good at PRESENTING.

To get someone started on creating a new habit, you may have to show by example first. YET, it's important to not limit their creative capabilities. In a good role play, they may surprise you with their creativity in creating a better way to START a new behavior. Don't over-instruct, provide guidance, but let them create a new way, a better way.

The real trick to role-playing is repetition. You may have to role-play the same scenario multiple times. Minor corrections, to instill a new skill to become a future habit, may require you to role-play the same scenario 3,4,5, even 6 times. Be patient!

When teaching a new skill through role-playing here's a simple formula I've found successful was originally taught to me by the Canadian thought leader on leadership development, Dr. Harvey Silver:

TEACHING A NEW SKILL

- SHOW THEM and TELL THEM what you are doing, and I mean every last part of it.

For example, let's pretend I'm teaching you how to build a paper airplane. I will start by describing every last fold - which corner do I start with, what direction do I fold it, how I crease the fold, talking through every single, last step

If this is a task related to a customer service or sales interaction, start with you playing their part, and let them be the customer - but while you are acting out your part, explain your part! Then act it out again, minus the explanation of what you're doing

- SHOW THEM and get them to TELL YOU

Let them state the instructions out loud, while you perform the actions. They should be just as specific, not leaving out any steps while you continue to demonstrate what they are telling you to do

If they mess up and forget a step, remind them what step was missed while you continue to show them following their directions

- SHOW THEM and get them to TELL YOU x 2

Repeat exactly, but this time, don't correct them - perform the steps exactly as they describe, just make the mistakes. If you end up with a non-functioning airplane then so be it. When they finish telling, you can back-step and remind them where they went wrong

- SHOW YOU AND TELL YOU

Now it's time for them to follow their own instructions and perform the new skill while speaking the instructions aloud. Feel free to correct as necessary, but get them to repeat it with the corrected instruction

- SHOW YOU AND TELL YOU X times?

Keep repeating this step until they can complete this new skill/talent/task without the need for your intervention or correction.

A reminder of the 3Ps of PRESENTING:

There are lots of other ways to practice. You're working on the skill right now, by reading this book. You're practicing. When it comes to effective communication and good presentation skills, there's no end to the number of videos on YouTube or TikTok to help you enhance your learning of how to present more effectively.

Communication, the ability to present, makes a massive difference in how your well-prepared coaching feedback is received. Investing in developing your presentation skills in general will help you in every other aspect of your career as it develops. Need to present in your next team meeting? Your boss asks you to prepare a presentation for the project you've been working on to present to her boss? Your client wants a summary of your company performance for the last quarter and you have to present a PowerPoint presentation at the next client review meeting? As your career develops the occasions you will need to present will continue to grow. Every opportunity to practice will continue to develop this essential skill that will support you for your entire career.

If you are interested in developing your presentation skills (and if you want to succeed in leadership, you should), I strongly recommend looking for a Toastmasters International group to join. Toastmasters is one of the world's largest organizations focused on improving communication and leadership skills through presentation. There are clubs in nearly every city on the planet and there are many clubs who meet online if meeting in person isn't an option for you. The benefit of Toastmasters is it requires you to do the presenting. Reading books and watching videos, while valuable, is nowhere near as valuable as actually DOING it.

Chapter 6: PRAISE

The single biggest mistake I've seen people make when coaching is not following up. Seriously, what was the point of spending all that time preparing, including evaluating, and presenting and having an amazing coaching conversation if you don't actually confirm it had any impact?? I'm truly bewildered at how so many otherwise good supervisors and managers don't follow up at all, let alone do it well.

What's the cause of missing follow-up? Not being clear up-front on WHY the coaching is happening and a clear HOW the coaching needs to happen. Remember, again - we are coaching to improve the 3Ps of Business (People, Product, Profit), which means we need to ensure the person we are coaching gets recognition and feels valued and appreciated! Following up is what is necessary if we want to give PRAISE and create that recognition and appreciation! Following up is necessary if we want them to feel valued. Following up is necessary if we want to keep our employees, keep them doing their job well to create a better product and help our business be successful. Follow up to give them PRAISE!

What's the best way to follow up?

1. Ensure you have shared the coaching summary with them if they were not able to take their own notes. This should NOT be everything you wrote, you don't need to include your prep work or your full evaluation summary - just what was discussed in the feedback discussion, the CONTINUE, STOP, START summary.

2. Observe them perform the same task you coached sometime within the next 48 hours, ideally without your direct supervision. If you must be over their shoulder, remember to try not to intervene - let them make their mistakes!

3. Take evaluation notes - but this time you are just specifically focusing on if they CONTINUED, STOPPED, and STARTED doing the things you coached - ignore everything else for the time being (except of course if you observe them breaking rules, cheating - this, of course, won't be for coaching but correction)

4. If they missed any part of your coaching, if they didn't Continue, Stop and Start what was discussed, then it's time to have a follow-up and reset conversation. This can be brief and informal - heck, if chat or email is your go-to way to have a quick conversation, that's fine - it doesn't have to be a big conversation unless they need help role-playing what you

were hoping they were going to start doing. Remember as the coach, your job is to support them in whichever way they need support. If they need a more detailed conversation, then make time for them and support them.

- FOLLOW UP AGAIN - RE-EVALUATE and make sure you're able to observe the behaviours which were coached

- NOTE - if this requires more than 3 repeated attempts to evaluate and identify the desired changes in behaviour, then something is wrong and will require a deeper conversation to understand why they aren't able to apply the learning. I recommend getting help from your boss, coach, or mentor when you run into this type of situation. This is the situation where they are either unwilling (low will issue) or do not have the capacity to do it (low skill issue) Until you are an expert, experienced coach, these conversations are exceptionally difficult and can damage the relationship you are trying so hard to build. See Chapter 8 for a more detailed explanation on how to handle these types of conversations.

5. When you can CONFIRM they have demonstrated the coached behaviours - now is the time to celebrate. This is what it was all about. Remember when I stated the desired result of coaching...this is it, to give the person you are coaching true PRAISE.

William James, educator and the first psychologist in North America, taught this important tenet:

"The deepest principle in human nature is the craving to be appreciated."

In my career, I've had the privilege to work directly with 10s of THOUSANDS of people from all across the globe. I've had the opportunity to see firsthand the impacts of both good and bad leadership. Leadership that inspires and informs people to enable growth, improvement, and happiness - and leadership that doesn't, by skipping feedback-based coaching & dolling out the wrong kinds of praise.

Turns out there is actually a good way to give praise. When delivered correctly, praise can uniquely fulfill our 'craving to be appreciated' while also encouraging behaviours that will help us grow and improve.

PRAISE RESEARCH

In the early 90s, Dr. Carol Dweck's research at Stanford University revealed how different types of praise affect children's mindsets.

They gave a large group of kids an IQ test, and then praised one group for their intelligence, and another group for their effort. When offered a choice of tasks afterward, most kids praised for intelligence chose easier tasks, while those praised for effort chose harder ones.

They then performed a second, similar IQ test. The intelligence-praised group's performance dropped, whereas the effort-praised kids, their performance improved significantly.

This study highlights the difference between a fixed mindset, where we see our abilities as unchangeable, and a growth mindset, where we focus on effort, improvement - PROGRESS.

Praising qualities attached to a person's identity can lead to a fixed mindset, making us risk averse.

In contrast, praising behaviors, effort, and persistence fosters a growth mindset, encouraging us to embrace challenges and improve.

MY PERSONAL PRAISE RESEARCH

I coached youth hockey and baseball for 10 years. Of course, I ensured I did not hand out participation trophies that weren't attached to recognition of accomplishment or effort.

I did my best not to praise labels attached to my player's qualities by saying things like "Josh, you're an amazing hockey player". If I had, I would have set kids on a path of a fixed mindset, incentivizing them to avoid risk and avoid failing.

Instead, I gave praise based on their effort on the ice, their behaviors, their persistence, "Josh, you really skated hard out there, especially when in a race for the puck". As a result, they started to believe in their capacity to improve, developing a growth-mindset.

Neuroscience, not just psychology, further supports the tenets of growth-mindset. Research has shown that our brain changes, creates new neural pathways, and even grows in size when we exhibit effort and overcome challenges. The brain itself can change, can improve.

When it comes to providing praise, I highly recommend acting like a gardener who wants his plants to grow.

If you want your plant to thrive, you'll need to plant it in a precise location to ensure the optimal temperature and access to sunlight.

But you'll need to give it personal attention, the right mix of water and nutrients for that particular plant's growth.

And of course, it needs to be attended to promptly, if we delay too long, our plant will wither away.

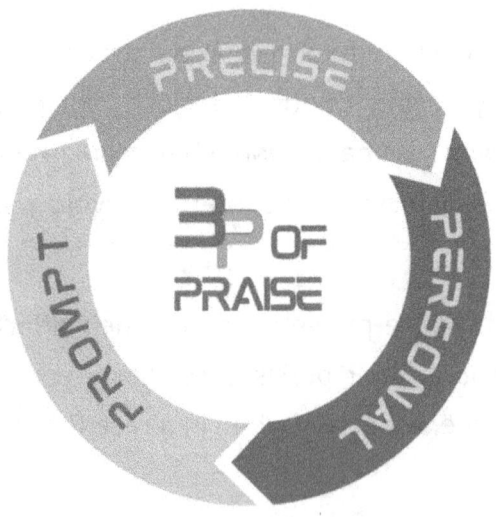

1st P of Praise – PRECISE

Praise won't be properly appreciated unless the person you are giving it to knows exactly what they are being praised for...you can't just tell someone, "Good job today" if they don't know what exactly they did that was good.

To give PRECISE praise, they need to know exactly what behaviors and effort they are receiving praise for. The world isn't suffering from a lack of praise, it's that we're bombarded with the wrong praise or empty praise like "thanks for being you", "You rock", "You're a rockstar". It's like white noise. As pointed out in the research on developing a growth-mindset, this kind of praise may have the opposite of our intended impact.

In your case, because it was clear about what behaviours you were coaching, what you helped them CONTINUE, STOP and START, the person you are giving praise to knows exactly what you are recognizing them for.

Consider just how powerful this is. To make Praise specific. Not a pizza party for everybody because "you guys are awesome". Precise praise for something they did, praise for something that has a direct impact on how they do their job. The kind of praise each of us truly craves.

Precise praise for behaviors, effort, persistence - PROGRESS.

2nd P of Praise – PERSONAL

Getting praise from someone you have no relationship with won't have near the impact as from someone you have a close relationship with. As their boss, who has demonstrated you care about the person and their success, it's nearly automatic that your relationship with that person is an important one to them. To quote Dr. Seth Silver & Timothy Franz from their book, "Meaningful Partnership at Work" about the relationship between bosses and their employees, "...your relationship with them is perhaps the single biggest factor in their experience at work". The stronger the quality of your relationship with them, the more meaningful your praise of them will be.

Now here's where you can assemble your praise to be more meaningful. If you have been capturing everything you know about this person, you can **personalize** the praise. How exactly do they like receiving praise based on your developed understanding of them as a unique person?

One of the most successful books in history is Dale Carnegie's "How to Win Friends and Influence People", selling over 30 MILLION copies worldwide. In that famous book, Carnegie writes "If out of reading this book you get just one thing: to think always in terms of the other person's point of view, and see things from his angle".

This is especially true when giving Praise. If you know what's important to them, now would be a good time to reiterate WIIFT (what's in it for them) because they implemented the coaching you provided. Including WIIFT that you know is aligned with their goals!

Remember the PLATINUM RULE – Treat others the way THEY wish to be treated!

How did catching them doing it right make YOU feel? Sharing your pride in their accomplishment, how it made you feel will not only make the praise more meaningful, but it will also strengthen your relationship, your connection with them.

The more personal we make the praise, the more impactful it will be.

3rd P of Praise – PROMPT

For praise to have maximum impact, you should deliver it immediately after observing the action. If I gave you praise today for something you did last month, it won't be near as impactful versus giving you praise for something you did 5 minutes ago. Because you observed the changed behaviour and immediately told them how happy you were to see the change, the praise has more value.

Too often, people think they need to hold back praise, to wait for the optimal moment. The reality is, it serves no purpose to hold back praise waiting for the perfect moment – see it, say it.

That's it folks - that's the 3Ps of Coaching (for 1-on1 on-the-job performance that is!)

Start with the PURPOSE of the coaching and the what

1. WHY: To improve the 3Ps of the business by helping them grow and improve in their job in the business

2. WHAT: Create an opportunity for PRAISE

PREPARE

- PROFILE
- PREVIEW
- PROBE

PRESENT

- POINT
- PRACTICE
- PRESENCE

PRAISE

- PRECISE
- PERSONAL
- PROMPT

In the next chapter, we'll talk about how frequently you should be coaching your team and how long you should plan on coaching sessions to take.

3P Coaching – A Summary & Recap

1st P of Coaching - PREPARE:

What do I do first? Start with WHY!

Knowing why you are coaching is important as it guides you through the rest of the process...and the answer to why you are coaching is always the same:

WHY we coach is that we want the person we're coaching to GROW and IMPROVE and to be motivated to keep doing 'it' - 'it' being whatever it is that we're coaching. How we coach will not only help the *person* we're coaching but referring to the 3Ps of a business, the coaching will improve the *product* (or service) we are delivering to our customer and ultimately the *profit* of the business we're coaching for. Why we coach is to improve ALL of the 3Ps of the BUSINESS!

WHAT we do, is use coaching to create an opportunity to create recognition and appreciation by giving PRAISE - To quote the philosopher and psychologist, William James:

"The deepest principle in human nature is the craving to be appreciated."

Remember it's important that we start with this in mind - that the purpose of your coaching is a sincere desire to help the person grow and improve. What we're doing when we coach is creating an opportunity to give the person you're coaching **praise**.

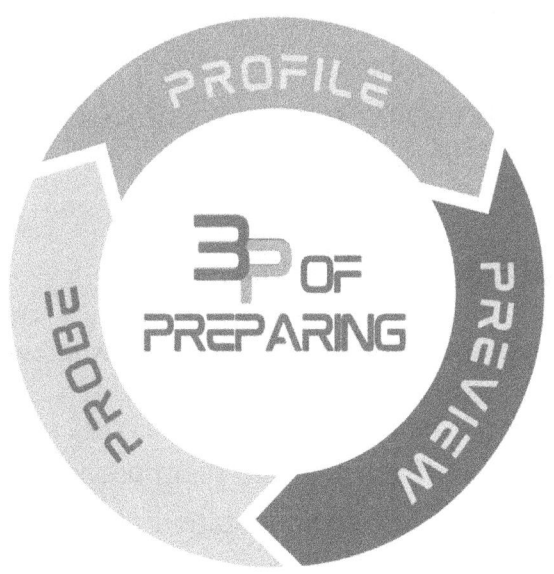

PREPARE➔*PROFILE*!!!

What do you know about the person you are coaching? Remember we NEVER use this information in any way that would conflict with being inclusive. It's meant to demonstrate that you know their story and their goals! What's important to them!! What they share when you asked them to tell *their* story

- What generation do they identify with? GenX, Millenial, GenZ?

- How long have they worked for the business?
- How long have they been doing their current job?
- What type of work did they do previously?
- What level of education did they achieve and what did they study?
- Did they share their family structure? Who's important to them?
- What do they like to do when they're not at work?
- What are their goals?

PREPARE→*PREVIEW*

- If you coached them previously, what was it you coached?

    o Important!! If you coached them previously, it better be documented....no documentation means you have nothing to follow up on, which means you wasted their time and yours!

    What is their past performance?

    o Are there reports, or metrics to review?

    o Importantly, what has been the trend of their results - have they been improving, declining, or flat-lined?

- Have some way to take notes. No notes, no coaching!
- From this information you should have a clear understanding of what FOCUS POINT you want to

ensure you follow in your coaching during the next step!

PREPARE→*PROBE!*

You will need to base your coaching on an evaluation of their current capabilities. Perhaps you can review their documented work, maybe there's a recording of their work if they are in a job like customer service, or you will just have to watch them perform their work live. But to coach, you need to evaluate them doing the actual job.

- Check yourself - you're not going to evaluate everything - remember in the PREVIEW step you identified a **FOCUS POINT** for this coaching. If you're coaching a barista at Starbucks and you are trying to help them make a Chai Tea Latte faster, don't worry about identifying behaviours related to how they smile at the customers.

- Make notes...regardless of what is being evaluated...think of a +/- or pros/cons list...include both observed behaviours and missing behaviours.

- BE SPECIFIC...you are trying to identify BEHAVIOURS...behaviours are things people SAY or DO...results are just that, results...you can't coach results, only behaviours.

  o Eg...RESULT: " stop making customers angry" vs BEHAVIOR: "stop calling customers jerks"

- Ultimately you want to end up with 3 lists:
  - Behaviours to CONTINUE (good habits)
  - Behaviours to STOP (bad habits)
  - Behaviours to START (missing good habits)
- Prioritize the list! You can't coach EVERYTHING you observed:
  - Of the behaviours you want to CONTINUE...pick one, the best one
  - Of the bad habits, pick ONE and only one..the worst one they should STOP, the biggest thing messing up potential success
  - Of the missing behaviours, things that could be added, that they should start...pick ONE that you'll help them role play so they can figure out a better way

2nd P of Coaching - PRESENT

Can't I just send them my notes? No! They need COACHING, an opportunity to clarify, discuss, and create a dialogue with you.

This means that you need to be good at PRESENTING.

To present effectively, we need to ensure three things – the 3Ps of Presenting – have a POINT, PRACTICE and PRESENCE – the art of speaking with more than our words – and LISTENING!

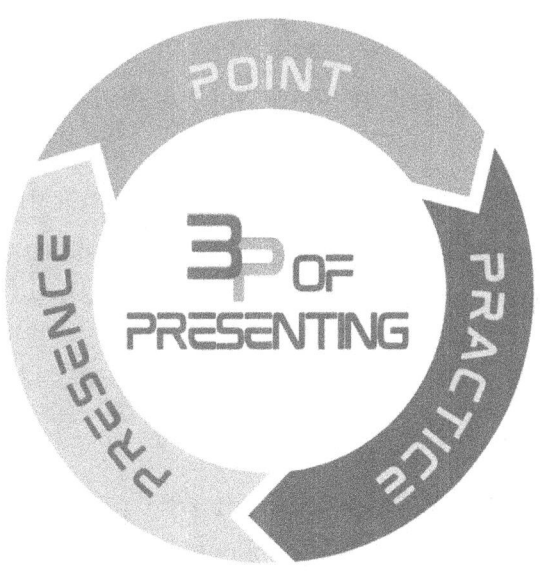

Again, this is a book on coaching, so let's stick to how to apply those 3Ps of Presenting – as it relates to COACHING!

PRESENT→*POINT*

Our POINT that we present to the person we're coaching needs to be aligned with this purpose of coaching as well as what we know about the person when we *PROFILED* them. Our POINT should then focus on the specific FOCUS POINT that will help them grow and improve in their job and WHAT'S IN IT FOR THEM to keep them motivated which we discovered when we *PREVIEWED* their performance. Lastly, our POINT should translate what we discovered when we *PROBED* their actual performance by evaluating their current work in action.

PRESENT→PRACTICE

What do I mean by practice? Well if you're just starting out coaching, why start practicing live? Why not practice in front of a mirror what you're going to say? Or better yet, practice your prepared coaching with your boss before trying it live with an employee. Ask your boss to take notes, and give you coaching on your coaching *before* you dive in head first.

PRESENT→*PRESENCE*

The third key to presenting well is to present with *presence.* You've invested significant time and energy to get ready to have the coaching conversation. You've prepared. You have a clear point to make in your coaching. You've practiced what you are going to coach. But if you want your message to be well-received you'll need to present with *PRESENCE.* While this isn't a keynote speech at a Ted Talk conference in front of 1000 people, how you present – your tone of voice, your body language, and paying attention to your audience still matters – even in a coaching session. As a coaching session, paying attention to the person you are coaching – LISTENING - is going to be more important than what you have to say. Providing opportunities for them to speak and proactively listening to THEM is how you present with *PRESENCE* while giving coaching feedback.

Here's a quick refresh on the steps to PRESENTING coaching feedback:

POINT - ensure you have reviewed your notes and present them to ensure you make your POINT clear

PRACTICE – Do a run through what you want to say, try it in front of the mirror, record yourself on your phone, or have your boss pretend to be the person you're coaching

PRESENCE – adjust your tone of voice, pay attention to your body language and remember to LISTEN

For the actual flow of the coaching conversation:

1. SMILE - Start a conversation with them that's light and friendly - please make sure you're smiling!
2. POINT – Introduce what the POINT of the coaching is going to be.
3. CONTINUE - Discuss one behaviour they should continue
4. STOP - The ONE behaviour to STOP and WHY it's hurting their performance!! Remember – this is NOT a 'Correction conversation' – you are providing helpful feedback, not a warning!
5. START - The ONE behaviour to START with ROLE PLAYING that they create

6. WIIFT - Discuss What's In It For Them (WIFFT)
7. RECAP and CONFIRM understanding
8. THANK THEM, remind them you are here to support them, and tell them you appreciate spending the time talking with them

3rd P of Coaching – PRAISE – The Cornerstone

What was the first step we discussed as we started to *PREPARE* to coach – even before we knew who we are going to coach? To understand WHY we coach at all, of course. We are coaching so that we can help our team GROW and IMPROVE to achieve what's in it for them (WIIFT) by creating an opportunity to give them PRAISE!

If we've done a good job so far, if we've **PREPARED** – by **profiling** who we will coach and their goals, **previewed** their past performance, **probed** their current performance, we then **PRESENTED** with a clear **point** to the coaching, **practiced** what & how we'll coach and delivered the coaching with **presence** – we're now in a position to do the most important thing – catch them doing it **RIGHT!** And when we do, we will make sure we give them ***PRAISE!***

But giving praise can be done well, mediocrely or even poorly. If we want to ensure we maximize the value of all of our efforts to get to the point where we can catch them doing it right, and give praise – praise that makes them feel appreciated, valued, motivated – we should ensure we do it well. Giving good praise requires you to follow the 3Ps of Praise – PRECISE, PERSONAL and PROMPT! The final cornerstone of the 3P Pyramid of success.

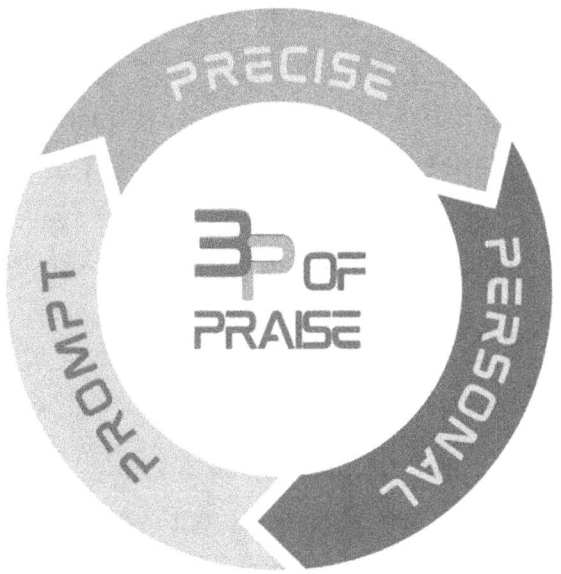

PRAISE→*PRECISE*

When we do catch someone doing something right and want to give them praise, we need to communicate precisely what we are giving them praise for. It should be SPECIFIC! While a general 'thank you' or 'good job' is nice, if they don't know why you're thanking them it doesn't carry much weight. The great news is, because we invested in doing our coaching well, we know exactly what behaviours we wanted them to CONTINUE, STOP and START doing. So when we **follow up** after their coaching and review their work, we know exactly what to watch or listen for. And when we give them *praise* we can be precise about what behaviour we're giving them – and they'll know exactly what we're talking about!

PRAISE→PERSONAL

No two people are the same. That's why the first step as we started preparing to coach someone was to understand their **PROFILE.** People have unique goals, they value WHAT'S IN IT FOR THEM (WIIFT) differently. This is why pizza parties are not the ideal form of praise – not everybody likes pizza!! Follow the 'PLATINUM rule' – treat others the way THEY wish to be treated.

PRAISE→*PROMPT*

The sooner the better. Follow up after your coaching quickly so you can catch them doing it right. And don't wait, when you catch them – give them precise and personal praise. Better late than never, but never late is better. Again, if we wait for their year-end annual performance review to doll out praise, it won't create a meaningful connection!

Here's the ideal steps to follow-up to ensure you create an opportunity to celebrate your coaching with **PRAISE** that's *precise*, *personal* and *prompt*.

- Share the Coaching Summary with the person you coached
- Observe them perform the same task
- Take follow-up evaluation notes

- Catch them doing it right! Lavish that praise on them.
    - PRECISE – they'll know exactly what they are getting praise for
    - PERSONAL – they know exactly WIIFT (what's-it-it-for-them) & how it made you feel
    - PROMPT – it just happened!

If you weren't able to catch them doing it right:

- Have a follow-up conversation. (repeat & reconfirm the desired Continue, Stop, Start behaviours)
- FOLLOW UP AGAIN - RE-EVALUATE and make sure you're able to observe the behaviours that were coached
- Identify if there is a SKILL vs WILL issue (possibly this becomes a CORRECTION conversation - more on this later)
- When you confirm they have demonstrated the coached behaviours - now is the time to celebrate – and give them the praise they earned!

That's it folks, that's the overall summary of the 3P Pyramid of Success that represents a successful business – all supported by the skills that are utilized to deliver effective coaching. The more you do it, the better you will get. The more PERSISTENTLY you learn about each level of the 3P Pyramid of Success that supports a business, the more successful you'll be. The more you develop the foundational skills of coaching, the better a coach you'll be. As mentioned in the 3Ps of Presenting, if you **PRACTICE** by having someone EVALUATE your coaching and provide *you* FEEDBACK on the quality of your coaching, that's where you will see your biggest improvements. We all need coaches, especially coaches themselves. Experience is said to be the best teacher, but Evaluated Experience is even better.

For a downloadable visual summary of the 3Ps of Coaching, visit www.3psolutions.ca/books-courses/praisedownloads.

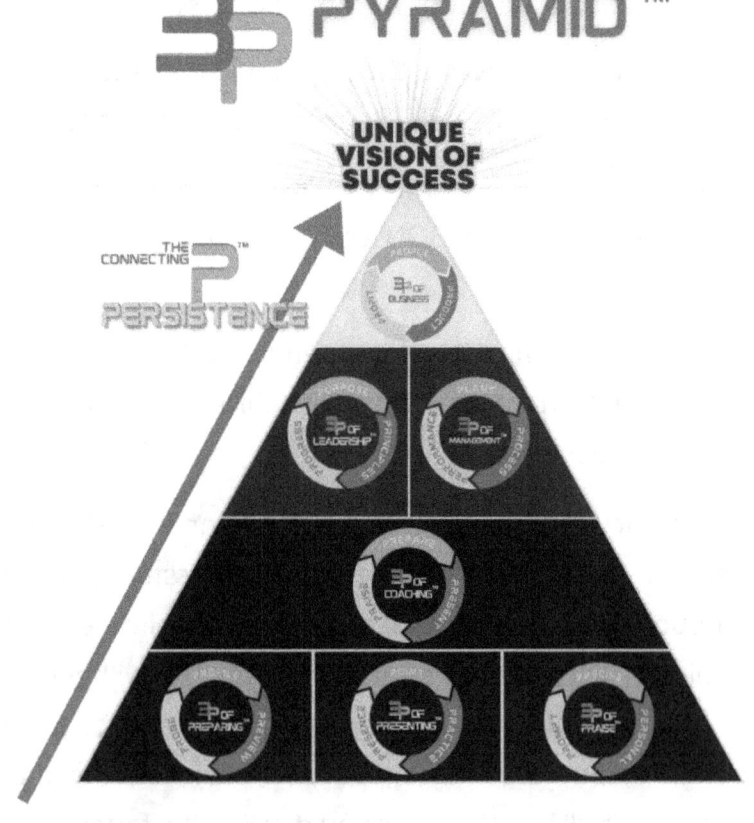

Chapter 7: Frequency & Duration of Coaching

Ok, so now I know that I can coach, why I'm coaching and how to coach to that desire result of catching them doing it right to give them PRAISE - but you may be wondering - how long should a single coaching session last and how often do I need to do them with my team members??? Short answer - it depends! It depends on what is being coached, the skill level of who is being coached and the complexity of the task that's being coached. This will all impact the duration of a single coaching session.

Depending upon how long one single coaching session takes will impact the frequency of coaching required.

One other important factor is how many members you have on your team - your time is limited, and it should be prioritized based on who needs coaching the most but you shouldn't neglect to coach your best performers either.

Remember, the desired result of coaching is to create an opportunity to provide PRAISE so that team members can feel appreciated...by you! That's the only way to achieve the PURPOSE of coaching - to improve the 3Ps of the business – including helping that person improve!

All that said, there are some basic rules of thumb that I'd suggest you follow:

Duration of a single Coaching session

Approximately 60-90 minutes

- Profile review of the person being coached – 2 minutes

- Preview of previous coaching & reporting of their performance to identify a Focus Point – 5 minutes

- Probing evaluation – 15-30 minutes (however long it takes to watch/review the person doing the task being evaluated, while documenting and summarizing what you want them to CONTINUE, STOP, START)

- Presentation of feedback – 30-45 minutes. Any longer than 45 minutes in a single coaching feedback session (not including follow-ups) is likely too long. Even if the task being coached is one that takes longer than that, you aren't trying to coach everything – you want to focus on just the specific habits you want to CONTINUE, STOP and START related to the point of focus...

1. SMILE – 2-5 minutes to open a coaching session - a bit of friendly how's it going, genuine interest in how they feel about their responsibilities, how things are going outside of work, building on getting to know them as a unique person and what their unique motivation is - why are they doing this job in the first place – building on the PROFILE you're keeping track of

2. POINT - 1 minute to review performance and discuss what the point of focus was for the evaluation you performed and why – how it will help them by making sure you've clearly let them know what the expected outcome for them this coaching will create

3. CONTINUE - 2 minutes to review and specify what good behavioural habit – in a dialogue - you want to see them **continue**

4. STOP - 2-5 minutes to review and clarify what bad habit you identified if they **stopped**, would immediately have an impact on their performance relative to the FOCUS POINT. Remember, this is a discussion. Getting to the WHY, asking 'why' three times to understand why they are doing this will help influence the change in behaviour

5. START - 10-30 minutes to review, practice, role-play the new habit you hope they **start** - this could go as long as 45 minutes if it is particularly challenging change - a good role-play practice takes as long as it needs, to demonstrate they understand when and how to implement this new best practice. Remember, this is something they weren't already doing - it's a new skill - this should be the longest part of the coaching session. Also remember, they are doing the creating and most of the talking here. But don't stop until they've nailed it!

6. WIIFT - 2-3 minutes to discuss, remind and reinforce the WIIFT - what's in it for them if they use this new behaviour in their next task

7. RECAP – 1-2 minutes to recap what needs to Continue, Stop and Start and the desired result of this coaching

8. THANKS – 1 minute to thank them for their time, for being a part of the team and for committing to continuous improvement and reassuring them that no matter what, you are always there to support them

- Follow-Up Evaluation – 15-30 minutes - As we can be laser-focused on observing the specific behaviors we wanted to see them continue, stop and start doing.

- Praise – 1 minute - Once we catch them doing it right, the actual giving of praise that's PRECISE - because they KNOW what they're getting praise for because we were clear on what they should to Continue, Stop and Start doing. It's PERSONAL because it's coming from YOU, their boss, you've shared WIIFT and what's important to them and you've shared how it made you feel. And of course you delivered it PROMPTLY, it can all be delivered in ONE MINUTE. While it's the MOST IMPORTANT step, the CORNERSTONE of this entire coaching model, to only take a minute. It's the step that will make them feel satisfied with the coaching, valued as an employee and happy with their own performance. But the actual delivery of PRAISE only takes a minute!

We may not even need to observe them doing the task from beginning to end to catch them doing it right. That said, if we do need to re-correct and adjust and follow up a second time, it will add a bit more time to following up.

Frequency

- A recurring coaching session can of course be incorporated into regularly scheduled 1-on-1's - in fact, I recommend whatever your schedule for 1-on-1's - that each 1-on-1 is an opportunity for a coaching session! Just don't forget to ensure 1-on-1's include you making sure they get an opportunity to tell you what support they need from you - or how YOU can improve in providing support

- No single team member should go more than ONE MONTH without a committed coaching session from you - no matter how big the team, how complex the tasks - going more than one month without an opportunity to receive PRAISE from good coaching is too long

- Unless there are SERIOUS performance issues, any more frequent than once per week (not including follow up sessions resulting from coaching) is likely not necessary if you've been providing good coaching - remember the result of your coaching is meant to influence and change BEHAVIOURAL HABITS - which means they need at least a little bit of time and follow up to sink in. Coaching more frequently than weekly will make it difficult to turn a coached behaviour into a habit

The best advice I have regarding setting the frequency of coaching is to prioritize your time and schedule the coaching that needs to be done - including the PREPARATION - the PROFILE REVIEW, PREVIEW of prior coaching and performance, PROBING evaluation & FOLLOW UP evaluation to catch them doing it right required to make the coaching complete to complete the coaching loop.

Essentially putting the 3Ps of Management into use! Remember the 3Ps of Management – PLANNING, PROCESSES and PERFORMANCE measurement? Now you get to apply your PLANNING and PERFORMANCE reporting skills to *prioritize* who you will coach and when, ensuring you expertly deliver your coaching PROCESS.

By prioritize (a very valuable planning skill) - I mean that you should put your newer or weaker team performers first into your coaching schedule - but as mentioned do NOT neglect your best performers - they want your praise as well! Not to mention, it's by evaluating and discussing performance with your best performers that you will continue to learn and improve your own knowledge. You can learn from anyone - including your weakest performers - but your best performers are the ones who can likely help you the most in being able to share best practices amongst your entire team.

It's vitally important for you to remember that while every coaching session is an opportunity for you to create a memorable event to give your team members PRAISE - they are also a learning opportunity for you as well. Of course, each time you coach, you will get better at PREPARING, PRESENTING, and following up on coaching with good PRAISE. But every coaching session also gives you an opportunity to learn more about your unique team members and what's important to them (building on their PROFILE) - AND - an opportunity to improve your own

133

knowledge about the skill/task you are responsible for coaching in the first place!

I also strongly recommend scheduling time proactively with your boss, leveraging the skill of PRACTICING to ensure you are getting an evaluation of your coaching. That you are receiving feedback from them, the *coaching* from your boss, on how you can continually improve your coaching through practice.

In the next chapter, we'll discuss those necessary, sometimes unpleasant conversations that happen between a boss and an employee – Correction Conversations.

Chapter 8: Correction Conversations

These are tough. Regardless of how many of them I've had - be it as a boss, a sports coach, or a parent, correction conversations are not fun for anyone - but they are crucial.

Correction is not the same as recurring 1:1 performance coaching. Performance coaching should always be a positive experience, initiated with the intent of creating an opportunity for giving out PRAISE. Correction conversations have a different purpose. But like anything worthwhile, as Stephen Covey, author of *'The 7 Habits of Highly Successful People',* says, "Begin with the End in Mind" - know why you are doing it.

Correction conversations are the ones that happen to prevent someone from being fired from a job. They happen because that person has done something there should be no tolerance for – PROHIBITED. Or they are doing something incorrectly due to not knowing expectations or carelessness – PERSONALITY. These could be issues like attendance, tardiness, dress code adherence, etc. The other type of personality issues are the result of something they have been repeatedly coached on yet are willingly choosing to do incorrectly, or due to the unfortunate fact they lack the capacity to do the job after repeated attempts to teach them – performance WILL vs SKILL issues.

Correction conversations could be about a poor attendance issue, a disregard for established and communicated rules or guidelines, or direct breaches of a code of conduct or an unwillingness or inability to do the job.

So, what is the purpose of a correction conversation? To restate, to reset expectations in clear terms that all agree if not addressed and corrected, will ultimately result in the end of their job or role with the organization.

We're assuming here that the conversation is necessary. It also assumes no rule is being broken to necessitate someone's immediate removal from the organization. Prohibited issues like theft or violence may not require a conversation, just a termination action.

If you think you've identified a PROHIBITED behaviour, my first recommendation is still to consult your boss, mentor, or Human Resources expert when you think a correction conversation is required. There is no point in guessing here. **Get help**! Not only is getting help here key to ensuring a correction conversation doesn't go off the rails, but this is also a great learning opportunity for you in your role as a supervisor or manager. Asking for help will strengthen your relationships with your boss or HR leader. In addition, it will provide a coaching opportunity for you to learn and grow as a leader.

If you are clearly addressing a PERSONALITY behaviour that has NOT been previously discussed with that person, then it's time to prepare to handle that conversation the right way. Again, I'll emphasize, when in doubt, GET HELP.

Once you're ready for the correction conversation, I still highly recommend being prepared to remain in complete control of your own emotions. Even if for an issue you consider minor – not following the dress code for example, it still has the possibility of becoming a difficult conversation. These are not conversations that should happen in the heat of the moment and even if they are, it's important that you are not emotionally charged leading the conversation - that could backfire on you in many ways, possibly jeopardizing your own position of responsibility. Not all correction conversations can get heated, a simple re-education of the dress code likely won't, but we should follow a consistent approach to any type of correction conversation.

One of the best books I've read when it comes to managing tough conversations is "Crucial Conversations" by a group of authors (Kerry Patterson, Joseph Grenny, Ron McMillan, Al Switzler). In their book, they insist that "The root cause of many – if not most - human problems lies in how people behave when others disagree with them about high-stakes, emotional issues". Based on my experience, nearly every CORRECTION conversation involves a situation where the person receiving the feedback will disagree with you, the result of the conversation is high stakes (keeping their primary source of income) and as a result, will likely be emotional.

This is why it's fundamentally important that you prepare by having support from HR or your boss and emotionally prepare yourself for a tough conversation. Once you've done that, here are the practical steps to managing through a correction conversation:

1. Ensure this is a private conversation. It should be done without an audience. Do NOT hold correction conversations in front of other team members. Remember the adage, *Praise Publicly, Correct Privately*

2. Get to the point. Don't beat around the bush, just state what was observed, when and by whom, and what rule was breached, what expectation is being missed, what mistake was made.

3. Confirm their agreement. If they claim they didn't do it, offer whatever proof but strive to get agreement. If they refuse to acknowledge the behaviour, if HR is not already directly involved, stop and get HR involved

4. Remind them you want them to be successful and that you are there to support them.

5. Document the conversation. Whatever system the organization uses for documentation, ensure a record of it is put there!

I'll repeat this one more time. If you think a behaviour requires a Correction Conversation, do NOT do this alone, especially if it's a new issue for you. Get help. Consult your boss, talk with HR, and ensure you have your facts straight.

Whatever you do, do not IGNORE problem behaviour. To quote Dr. Harvey Silver, "Problem behaviour ignored, is problem behaviour encouraged".

And hopefully, if we address the problem behavior with a good correction conversation, we will create an opportunity to see that person improve, and again, give ourselves an opportunity to give them PRAISE - that's PRECISE, PERSONAL and PROMPT.

The reality is, correction conversations are a type of coaching. It's just very important to distinguish from 1:1 Performance coaching.

A correction conversation still follows the 3Ps of Coaching - PREPARE, PRESENT, PRAISE - which ultimately makes us better leaders and managers to help us support the 3Ps of Business.

Chapter 9: Connection through Coaching & The 3P Success Pyramid

What's my Purpose

When I think of that first job as a paperboy, my early jobs working in restaurants and as a debt collector or my two decades years of executive leadership, and even now as I work on my own professional purpose as a consultant, and the purpose of this book – it's that I want to help make businesses and the leaders of those businesses more successful.

My personal belief is that business is the most fundamental and important engine that drives improvement for the world. Purpose-driven businesses, led by principled and progress-minded leaders - create abundance, opportunity, and prosperity for all of society. The most effective leaders are those who have control of their own time to focus that time where they truly desire.

If making businesses and leaders more successful is my purpose, understanding the most important values of leadership will help me better define my own mission, vision and values. The three fundamental values of leadership that I believe to be universally true to be effective leaders are that we need to:

1. **LEARN** - learn from our own experiences and learn from others - be it mentors, or others that have been successful. Heck, we can learn most from the things they failed at - regardless - leaders need to ensure they learn from both their own experiences and new ideas. Never stop learning. Learning makes us continuously better. Learning makes us better leaders. And we help others learn by being an effective coach.

2. **INNOVATE** - Not accepting the status quo, constantly searching to find new ways to improve upon and use improved systems or tools - striving for a better way is essential to success and strong leadership - or simply put - a need to constantly innovate.

3. **CONNECT** –as leaders – of a business or otherwise - connecting actions to desired results, connecting with customers, helping connect team members together, and ultimately connecting others with a shared Mission, Vision, Values, and Purpose (MVVP). To connect we need to apply those other universal

principles of kindness, truthfulness, and integrity – and our essential desire for PRAISE. Connection is why we strive to lead.

Learn, Innovate & Connect - those three words represent the most important values of leadership to me, they are related to my purpose - and ultimately the purpose of writing this book.

Based on my purpose, my WHY – helping businesses and their leaders achieve their unique vision of success, will create more abundance, opportunity, and prosperity for the world. And by applying the leadership values of Learn, Innovate and Connect, my mission becomes clearer.

My Mission: To help businesses and their leaders grow and optimize their time through learning, innovation and connection.

With that understanding of my mission in place...

My Vision: To be THE Enabler of Success FOR businesses and leaders WHO want to see their business go from good to great!

Diving a bit deeper into Connection

Countless books, inspirational motivational speakers, psychologists, sociologists, anthropologists, and even evolutionary biologists seem to agree – that we strive for connection, it's essential to why we are here.

Harvard University initiated a study in the 1940s involving 724 young men from a wide variety of backgrounds, whom they interviewed every two years – surveying them to understand their mental and physical health as well as their experiences in their careers, marriage, and quality of life. The team of researchers kept asking these questions of those same men for the next 75 years, including interviewing the spouses and children of those initial participants. What was the key finding of this continuous study carried on by 4 generations of researchers? It's good relationships that keep us both happier and healthier - not money or fame. Social connections with family, friends, and community are good for us, and loneliness is bad for us. The quality of those connections matter, and good relationships protect the body and the mind.

Given we will spend about 50 years of our lives in the workforce, working with other people, I'd suggest we may as well make the most out of this time and try to make some good relationships with the people we interact with at work - having strong connections with others actually matters!

If you're in a leadership role (or want to be in one), it means you need to get good at being a good boss - and the most effective way I can think of to be a good boss AND positively benefit the 3Ps of the business you're working in - is by being a good COACH. Knowing how to coach effectively, how to communicate effectively – to 'Inform, influence and INSPIRE the behaviour of others toward the progressive achievement of a worthy ideal' – coaching that PERSISTENTLY adheres to the 3Ps of coaching, those foundational skills that support the entire 3P Pyramid of success – PREPARE, PRESENT & PRAISE - not only will help your team deliver better profits for your company and a better product for your customers - it will also significantly help improve your relationship with your team members – the people that make up the business. It will strengthen your connections.

As I had mentioned at the beginning of the book, we are only tackling ONE specific type of coaching of the many different situations we will need to learn how to handle to be a great boss. Handling interviews, quarterly or annual reviews or advanced correction conversations will take additional learning to get you all the way there. These different situations will require modifications to how we coach. The foundational skills of the 3Ps of Coaching that support being a good leader and a good manager – that for every conversation we have with someone we're trying to build a connection with - we PREPARE, PRESENT and create opportunities to give PRAISE. These foundational skills can be applied in those different situations. These same foundational skills can be translated into how we have conversations with customers, peers, bosses, or investors. By applying these skills to the activity that you will do most frequently, regular 1-on-1 performance coaching with employees, you will develop how to apply these skills in those other situations.

We can lead better by treating people like someone who can choose to improve – choosing a growth mindset. Telling them you're confident that they can handle criticism and that you're confident they can improve will make the praise more valuable.

We truly have the power within us to lead business and society in a more positive direction. We have it within our ability to help people build the strength to overcome challenges and be receptive to hearing honest, sincere and caring feedback to help them and us both grow and improve. Please lead with me, help us inform, influence and inspire people, and start giving praise the way it should be given.

BTW - Humour is an important hack to making connections with people. Bringing a smile to the people you're working with is priceless. If you can incorporate humour and a smile into your coaching, do it.

It's all about connection folks.

Happy Coaching & Connecting with PRAISE!

www.ingramcontent.com/pod-product-compliance
Lightning Source LLC
Chambersburg PA
CBHW070430010526
44118CB00014B/1977